The Story of
RAF Madley

The Story of
RAF Madley

by

Fiona Macklin

Logaston Press

LOGASTON PRESS
Little Logaston Woonton Almeley
Herefordshire HR3 6QH
logastonpress.co.uk

First published by Logaston Press 2006
Reprinted 2007
Copyright © Fiona Macklin 2006

ISBN 1 904396 65 8   (978 1 904396 65 9)

Set in Times New Roman by Logaston Press
and printed in Great Britain by
Oaklands Book Services, Stroud, Gloucestershire

Front cover illustration: Dominie aircraft, as used at Madley for initial training
Rear cover: (top) From left to right, back row: Anthony Geer and Billie Lowrey; front row: Vic ?, unknown, Cyril la Bonne
(lower) A tongue in cheek photo taken around Christmas 1945, the shield motto was 'Get your finger out'!
Previous page: The 'Sparks' awarded to cadets on graduation to Wireless Operator Ground Crew

Contents

Acknowledgments

This book would not have been possible without the assistance of many individuals and organisations. Funding was provided by British Telecom and the Heritage Lottery Fund. Official documents, records and other publications were sourced from M.O.D., RAF Hendon, Imperial War Museum, National Archives, Hereford County Records Office, Hereford Sites and Monuments Records, Hereford City Museum and Library, Herefordshire Lore, Woolhope Naturalists' Field Club and Hereford Cathedral Library. I would like to thank the staff of these organisations for their assistance. Various other books to which I referred are detailed in the bibliography at the end of this publication.

Special thanks go to the veterans of RAF Madley, particularly all those who contributed photographs, memories and details of life on the base. So many of you offered information and anecdotes, but in particular I would like to thank Mr. E. Turner, Mrs. P. Evans, Mr. R.W. Tilyard, Mr. E. Griffiths, Mr. G. Meats, Mr. W. Owen, Mr. M. Stimson, Mr. G. Floyd, Mr. F. Day, Mr. E. Jackson, Mr. J. Thorn, Mrs. E. Lambert, Mrs. P. Pitt, Mrs. B. Macklin, Mr. E. Hunt, Mr. C. Davis, E. Bettinton, Mr. G. Pembridge, Mr. D. Lewis, Mr. W. Luffman, Mr. B.J. Godfrey, Mr. P. Perkin, Mr. A. Geer, Mr. G. Lamputt, Mrs. B. Pring Mill, Mr. P. Brewster, Mr. R. Payne, Mr. A. Patrick, Mrs. D. Elridge, Mr. G. Collett, Mrs. M. Dison, Mr. A. Badman, Mrs. R. Morgan, Mrs. B. Shackley, K.D. Daniels, Mr. L. Peek, Mr. K.P. Summerlin, J.H. Simmonds, Mrs. Harrison, Mrs. R. Cotton-Symonds and Mr. P. Rowe. A very warm thank you goes to Mr. Bill Williams who has contacted other veterans of RAF Madley and established an annual reunion. Without Bill's enthusiasm and fondness for Madley, this project would not have been so enjoyable. Thanks to Phil Evans, Trustee of Madley Environmental Study Centre (MESC), who provided invaluable information on the history of BT and MESC. Thanks also to Dilys Bowen and Maureen Venn for contacting many veterans and noting their stories. Maureen can also take the credit for working on the photographs and maps used in this publication. A huge thank you goes to Mr. Andy Johnson for his energy and enthusiasm, his meticulous attention to detail and fastidious revision of the manuscript. Andy has helped me avoid errors in fact and if any erroneous statement is herewith written it is my sole responsibility. And lastly, thanks to my mother, Rose Macklin, for proof reading and offering suggestions and providing numerous cups of tea!

Fiona Macklin
October 2006

Preface

In 2003 I noticed a letter from Bill Williams in the *Hereford Times* suggesting that there should be a memorial on the Madley Airfield, recognising those that had trained there and had subsequently lost their lives during the Second World War. I have been in contact with Bill since that day.

In 2004 Fiona Macklin was employed by MESC as a Project Officer, and being aware of Fiona's background at the Imperial War Museum and that she was also researching her own book relating to the Second World War, I asked Fiona to continue the research that had been started by MESC, with a view to publishing a book on RAF Madley.

In 2005 MESC held an event on the airfield to commemorate those involved during the war, a memorial sculpture of a Dominie plane was unveiled, and veterans of Madley Airfield and their families were invited as special guests, it was an opportune time to gather further information. With additional extensive research into wartime records by Fiona, it was now possible to publish a book as a tribute to everyone involved at RAF Madley.

All proceeds will be used to further the aims of MESC, providing environmental education to people of all ages and abilities. Information about these activities and developments can be found on the MESC website at www.mesc.org.uk

Phil Evans, Trustee MESC

Introduction

People have always been intrigued by flight. The ancient Egyptians worshipped bird-gods such as Horus and Bennu, there is the mythical phoenix rising from ashes whilst the Greek tale of Icarus soaring towards the sun is still a favourite children's story.

Today we live in a world where aircraft and flying are part of everyday life so it is very easy to forget that man-made flying machines only came into existence a little over 100 years ago. On 17 December 1903 brothers Orville and Wilbur Wright became the first men to fly a manned aircraft. Five years later in October 1908, Samuel Cody became the first man in Britain to fly in a powered aircraft, flying a total of 500 yards at Farnborough in Hampshire, near the site where in 1913 he tragically crashed and died. Just nine months after Cody's historic flight, Louis Blériot successfully piloted a mono-plane across the English Channel, landing safely on 25 July 1909. The age of flight was born.

The Army and the Royal Navy recognised that flying capabilities introduced a new concept into warfare, initially in the role of reconnaissance, and in April 1911 the Air Battalion of the Royal Engineers was formed at Larkhill. The Battalion's aircraft were limited to airships, balloons and kites, but it wasn't long before the role of aircraft was appreciated and in 1912 King George V signed a warrant to establish the Royal Air Corps, the forerunner of the Royal Air Force. The Royal Air Corps consisted of an Army Wing and a Naval Wing. The Wings were commanded by the service they represented and were answerable, as a consequence, to the War Office and the Admiralty respectively. The Army Wing oversaw all flight operations over land which required light, short range aircraft, whilst the Naval Wing's responsibility was for the shipping lanes and coastal defences that required longer range, heavier aircraft. This inevitably led to the two Wings designing their own aircraft and organising supplies, which together with a lack of a single overall Air Corps Commander, led to a split between the two Wings. The split became official in 1914 when the Naval Wing established its own Royal Naval Air Service. This compounded the problems of aircraft manufacture, supplies and training. It soon became obvious that a single air service was needed, and in 1917 the Air Forces (Constitution) Act was passed allowing for the creation of a new Air Ministry to sit as an equal beside the War Office and the Admiralty. The Air Ministry took several months to structure, organise and administer the new service, until on 1 April 1918 the Royal Air Force was established.

The formation of the RAF occurred during the latter stages of the First World War, the conflict that saw the advent of aerial attack. During 1918 the RAF dropped 5,500 tons of bombs on Germany and destroyed 2,953 enemy planes. Germany also had developed a strong air force, and their ace pilot, Manfred Albrecht Freiherr von Richthofen, otherwise known as the Red Baron, was responsible for shooting down over 80 allied planes. Other countries involved in the conflict also had developed aerial capabilities with France, Canada, South Africa, Australia, Ireland, Belgium, Austria-Hungary, Italy, USA and Russia all boasting ace pilots. However, at the end of the First World War, the Royal Air Force was recognised as the largest in the world.

After the war, development continued to improve the range and performance of aircraft. By June 1919 the first transatlantic flight was successfully completed from Newfoundland to Ireland, and in December the same year the first flight from England to Australia occurred. But despite these great advances in technology, the RAF was under threat. Severe cuts to the defence budgets after the war and disagreements between the Royal Navy and the Army threatened to disband the RAF as an independent service and absorb it within the two 'old' services. The RAF was to survive the defence cuts and political disagreements to remain a separate force, but the Army and Navy refused to allow the RAF to use the same rank titles; hence the ranks of Flight Lieutenant, Wing Commander etc.

The RAF continued to increase its personnel and aircraft. In 1931 two important aircraft were developed: the Tiger Moth and the Hawker Fury, the latter becoming an elite fighter aircraft until it was replaced by the iconic Spitfire. Test pilot 'Mutt' Summers flew the Spitfire on its maiden flight in 1936, and on landing told the aircraft's designers 'don't touch anything'! By 1934 concerns about Germany re-arming under Hitler's leadership prompted the decision to expand the air force to a total of 128 squadrons. News of Hitler's growing arsenal continued, and a year later the British Government voted to treble the number of military aircraft, an increase of 1,500. By 1936 the service had grown so large it was in need of reorganisation, so four Commands were introduced: Bomber Command; Coastal Command; Fighter Command; and Training Command. At the same time the RAF Reserve was formed which required personnel to attend training sessions conducted at weekends so as not to interfere with civilian occupations, and one fortnight camp per year. This strategy allowed an additional 63,000 men, already fully trained as pilots, technical or medical staff, to be called into full time service on 1 September 1939, a tremendous resource at the beginning of the Second World War. Just a day after Britain officially entered the war on 3 September 1939, the RAF suffered its first losses of the conflict when five Wellingtons were shot down. A war fought so much in the air and sustaining constant losses required a steady stream of personnel, trained air and ground crew, to replace those lost in battle. The RAF became crucial to the outcome of war.

RAF Madley No. 4 Radio School was established in 1941. The School trained cadets in the operation of wireless/telegraphy (W/T) systems to be used both on the ground and in the air. Once the cadets passed their examinations in Morse Code, Aircraft Recognition, Procedure and Technical, they would be awarded their 'flashes' and posted to destinations across the globe. This book tries to illustrate their days in training, their initiation into service life, and provide a glimpse into their world.

Village History

No. 4 Radio School was located near the village of Madley, 6.5 miles west-south-west of Hereford city. The site of the Radio School was determined by geology and practicality. Herefordshire is largely composed of Old Red Sandstone, 'red' because it was exposed to oxygen as it formed. Some 25,000 years ago the glaciers of the last Ice Age stretched from Scotland to the Brecon Beacons. As the ice moved steadily south it gouged out large tracts of land forming the sweeping hillsides of the Beacons and the Black Mountains. Around 17,000 years ago the climate warmed again causing the glaciers to melt, leaving behind the rock and sand caught within the ice. These deposits formed the hills that surround Madley, and provided the solid foundations to take the extreme weight of the runways and aircraft in the level plain at their feet.

The station site covered an area of approximately 300 acres, the perimeter of which was some 10 miles long. Although the station was dispersed over a large area, the majority of it was located along an old Roman Road called Stoney Street.

Prior to the Roman occupation, this fertile area was inhabited by tribal Britons. Five flints were discovered in a field near Madley in 1966 and evidence of bell-shaped 'Wessex' barrows has established that Bronze Age people inhabited the Madley region. There is also evidence of a henge site just outside Madley which dates from 2,500–2,000 BC. A further 18 Bronze Age burial sites have been discovered a few miles away in the Black Mountains. In the late Bronze Age and through the Iron Age, hill-forts were built that contained communities with streets along which timber round houses and stores were erected. Archaeological investigations have found bones of sheep, cattle and pigs indicating that these animals were farmed in the vicinity and probably kept on occasions inside the hill-fort, although there is evidence for farms themselves in the surrounding valleys. In Herefordshire, the largest hill-fort was located at Credenhill, across the River Wye from Madley. This fort covered approximately 50 acres and would have housed a relatively large population. Hill-forts have been discovered all around Madley: at Vowchurch a few miles to the south of the village, and at Eaton Bishop a mile to the east where the hill-fort was defended by a 3-metre high rampart. In 1981 a gold artefact dating from between 30 and 10 BC was found near Stoney Street.

The arrival of the Romans in 43 AD led to drastic changes in the hill-fort communities. Excavations of some hill-forts have unearthed human bones bearing the signs of a brutal death. One can only imagine the carnage that resulted from the battles between the trained and triumphant Roman soldiers and the local farming population of the hill-fort tribes. Certainly the population seems to have declined in number around the time of the Roman arrival.

The occupying Roman Legions required a vast amount of food which they could not grow or hunt for themselves, as their military duties were their first priority. The Romans also required horses for transport, tents for accommodation, and clothing. As Rome considered it owned all occupied land, the farmers in Britain had to pay Rome rent to farm the land, called a Tribute tax. The tax was often payable in corn, a staple diet of the Roman soldier. This resulted in the Herefordshire countryside being used increasingly for agricultural purposes, and techniques for harvesting and storing of grain became more sophisticated. Prosperity for those who had survived the invasion increased.

With the country unified under Roman rule, the need for defended communities diminished. New towns and villages were built on low lying land, often near a river. The towns usually comprised one or two main streets which were lined with rectangular wattle and daub houses that replaced the traditional wooden round houses of the hill-forts. Roman houses were frequently two stories with tiled roofs, and the more affluent owners could even install under-floor heating, mosaics and highly decorated walls. Public buildings for administration and local government were also a common feature of Roman towns, and larger communities had Baths where dignitaries and important men could relax, discuss business, or play games. In Herefordshire there are several Roman walled settlements. In addition to the main town of *Magnis* (Kenchester) across the River Wye from Madley, there were others at Leintwardine, Blackwardine near Stoke Prior, Stonechester near Leominster, Stretton Grandison and *Ariconium* near Ross-on-Wye, and their boundaries can clearly be seen from the air. *Magnis* was the most important Herefordshire Roman town. It was surrounded by a 2-metre thick wall of irregular shape, with four gates allowing entry. The town's main road was some 15 feet wide running east to west. There have been various finds at Kenchester including lead drainpipes, an oculist's stamp and coins, pottery and jewellery, mosaic floors and plastered walls. A highly decorative mosaic floor was removed and can be viewed at Hereford Museum and Library.

Roman villas also dotted the Herefordshire landscape, though little is known about these sites. It is rumoured that the foundations of a Roman villa were once uncovered at Madley near Stoney Street. Another rumour places a mosaic floor underneath the main runway at RAF Madley. However, neither of these stories has been substantiated. Villas have been located at Bishopstone, Putley, and Walterstone, where a villa with tessellated pavements was discovered on Stoney Street, but near the Monmouthshire border. Stoney Street linked the Roman fortress at Caerleon near Cardiff with Wroxeter, near Shrewsbury. South of the Wye it passed through *Gobannium* near Abergavenny. Once it crossed the Wye en route to *Magnis* it became known as Watling Street, and from *Magnis* turned north to pass through Leintwardine. In 1893 an area of the road was exposed during repairs at Abbey Dore railway station. The stone surface of the road was still intact just 18 inches below the surface of the soil. The stones used varied in size from 3 inches to 12 inches in diameter, and the width of the section of road excavated measured 12 feet 9 inches. Remarkably, the tracks from chariots or wagons were still clearly visible on one side of the road, but the other side had no evidence of wheel ruts at all. It may be assumed that this side was reserved for pedestrian use. The road also had evidence of being hastily constructed, as the joins between the stones were not of the usual high craftsmanship. Neither was the road curbed, unlike others in the Forest of Dean, nor did it have any drainage ditches running alongside. It can only be guessed at why the road was constructed in such a fashion; perhaps there was trouble elsewhere that called for the swift relocation of Roman troops. The comparatively poor construction had also resulted in a number of potholes that had been even more poorly repaired. The resulting rough finish would have ensured a very uncomfortable journey for wheeled transport, and, consequently, the archaeologists from the Woolhope Naturalists' Field Club who inspected the site concluded that Stoney Street was a secondary road, and that another road was probably the main link between the Roman forts in the north and south. Even so, there have been many Roman finds on Stoney Street and on the RAF site itself. A Roman coin, two Roman lamps and an urn were discovered near the station site. Pottery, glassware, bronze brooches, buckles, keys, tools and other artefacts have been found throughout the area. Many can be viewed at Hereford City Museum.

The Roman Empire came under increasing pressure from population movements to its east, and in the early 400s AD troops were gradually removed from Britain to the Continent to try and help stem the flow. By 410 the Roman Empire ceased to rule in Britain. The cohesive social structure that had developed broke down once the unity that had been enjoyed under a common Roman leadership disappeared, and Britain became divided into small individual kingdoms that competed for dominance. Madley became part of the kingdom of Ergyng and it is thought that during the late 5th century, the name of Madley came into existence.

One of the kings of Ergyng was known as Pebiau, or Claforawg in the ancient British tongue. Legend says that Pebiau returned home after an expedition waging war on his enemies to find his unmarried daughter, Ebrdril, pregnant. In fury he ordered his daughter be stuffed into a sack and thrown into the River Wye, but instead of drowning she washed ashore. Exasperated by his daughter's good fortune the king then ordered her to be burnt

alive. A huge funeral pyre was built and Ebrdril was thrown upon it. The next morning the king expected to find the charred remains of his wayward daughter, but instead found her alive and well, and nursing a baby boy. Drawn towards the infant despite his hostile feelings towards his daughter, Pebiau was touched on the face and lips by the baby's hands, instantly curing him of an ailment, thought to be leprosy, which caused his mouth to dribble uncontrollably. Pebiau forgave his daughter and named the boy Dyfrig, Dubricius in Latin, and named his birth place *Madd* meaning 'good' and *Lle* (ley) meaning 'place' or 'clearing'. Pebiau also bestowed a gift of land upon Dyfrig, who grew into a very learned man, founding a monastic settlement and seat of learning at Hentland or Llanfrother, above the Wye near Hoarwithy. When this site became threatened by the Saxons, the story goes that Dyfrig was visited by an angel who told him that he must construct a new building at a 'place of pigs'. The next day Dyfrig saw a white sow suckling her piglets, and on that spot he laid the first foundation stone of a monastery. Today the location is known as Moccas, meaning 'place of pigs'. (This appears to have been quite a usual sign, as many a religious site owes its location to such visions and the subsequent sighting of a sow.)

Britain remained divided into kingdoms, but within a few decades of the arrival of the Saxons and the Angles from the Continent the smaller kingdoms were incorporated into the larger powerful later kingdoms of Northumbria, Wessex, East Anglia, Essex, Sussex, Kent and Mercia. The kingdom of Ergyng was split in two, the River Wye forming a natural boundary. Land to the north of the river was absorbed into the kingdom of Mercia which was established in circa 585 AD, whilst that to the south remained the territory of native Britons and became known as Archenfield. The Saxons brought their own brand of paganism with them, but the local population remained mainly Christian, which it had become in the latter years of Roman rule. There is evidence of both religions at Madley, as traces of Celtic and Saxon graves have been found behind the village hall. By 660 the king of Mercia had converted to Christianity. Like the Romans before them, the Angles and the Saxons had frequent skirmishes with the British/Welsh along the border, especially as Mercia pushed its territory westwards, which it tended to do more adjacent to what became northern Wales, Archenfield appearing to act as a sufficient and independent buffer hereabouts. In 757 King Offa of Mercia ordered a massive earthwork be constructed through the Welsh hills. Controversy surrounds this undertaking: was it meant to mark a border, perhaps being patrolled by horseman to check on any potential threat from Wales? If so, why did it need to be built within yards of the already existing Wat's Dyke in places, and in any event Mercia had pushed its boundaries even further west within a few years of its construction. Was it built from sea to sea, as affirmed by the chronicler, Asser? If so, why is it largely absent in Herefordshire and fragmentary further south? The parts of dyke that survive indicate that it would have consisted of a ditch approximately 2 metres deep on the side facing Wales, and a bank of earth about 6 metres high and up to 20 metres wide. A dyke lies just a couple of miles from Madley near the River Wye at Bridge Sollers, but there is dispute as to whether this earthwork is part of Offa's Dyke or some other territorial marker.

The Dyke may have protected the Saxon kingdom of Mercia to the west, but another enemy came from the east, the Vikings. A great Danish army landed in 864 AD and soon all but one English kingdom fell to the Vikings as they rampaged across the country. Alfred, King of Wessex, managed to stave off the Viking attacks, but the Vikings sailed their long boats up the Rivers Severn and Wye to attack Mercia. The kingdom was partitioned; the Vikings controlled east Mercia across England to the North Sea, while the Saxons controlled west Mercia, the city of Hereford, and Archenfield including Madley. This partition did not stop the Vikings conducting raids into Saxon and Celtic territory. In 914 AD the Vikings ravaged Archenfield and took the bishop hostage, only releasing him when the king paid a ransom. Battles between the Vikings, the Saxons and Welsh continued for many years during which time Hereford castle and city were fortified and expanded. The Earl of Hereford, Harold Godwinson, took control of Hereford castle after a devastating attack by the Welsh under the command of Gruffydd ap Llewellyn in 1055, which saw large parts of the city burnt to the ground. Harold later became king of England upon the death of Edward the Confessor. The Saxon era ended when Harold was defeated by the Normans at the Battle of Hastings in 1066.

Like the Romans and Saxons before them, the Norman victors recognised the danger of the Welsh, and wasted no time in building a series of castles and fortified sites along the border. Large castles were built at Shrewsbury, Ludlow and Chepstow to act as strongholds of Norman power, bolstered by a plethora of smaller enterprises. Over the succeeding decades approximately 120 castles and fortified sites were constructed in Herefordshire, including a small motte and bailey castle north-west of Madley church. The motte, which appears to have been of sufficient size to have carried a shell keep, seems to have been removed in 1963, whilst much of the bailey has succumbed to modern development.

The church, initially built of wood, was replaced around 1100 with a stone-built cross-shaped church that contained one of the largest stone fonts in Britain. Over time the church was expanded, and in the 13th century a tower was added. The walls, like those of nearby Dore Abbey built in 1147, were vibrantly painted. The church was originally dedicated to Ebrdril, mother of Dyfrig, but later became dedicated to the Blessed Virgin Mary. A statue of the Virgin Mary within the church became the object of pilgrimage and attracted many donations, money that financed the building of the semi-octagonal chancel. Some of the Norman parts of the church remain today, notably the western end of the nave and the north porch. The church has a late medieval crypt, the fine 14th-century Chilstone chapel in the Decorated style, six bells, some of the finest stained glass in England, and seating for an optimistically large congregation of 1,500.

In the meantime Hereford became one of the largest towns in England, partly due to the existence of what became an extensive castle that was usually retained in royal hands and that acted as a base in the wars against the Welsh, but also due to the presence of the remains of two saints in the cathedral — St. Ethelbert, former king of East Anglia; and St. Thomas, a former bishop of Hereford canonised in 1320. The cathedral's chained library ensured the city became a major centre of learning, rivalling Oxford and Cambridge. But the city's size and importance meant that it sometimes attracted attention of the wrong variety, which had repercussions on the surrounding countryside. In 1139 Hereford Castle and Cathedral became embroiled in the civil war between Stephen and Matilda, who both claimed to be the rightful heir to the English throne. In 1265 another dispute for the crown between Simon de Montfort and Henry III saw the castle used as a prison when Simon kidnapped Henry and his son Edward, and held them prisoner there. For a while Simon ruled the country from Hereford. Once Edward had taken the throne as Edward I and subsequently battered the Welsh into submission and hemmed them in with the latest in castle construction, Hereford's importance started to decline.

Madley village settled into a relatively peaceful farming existence, with the population concentrating on farming, growing barley, hemp, flax, parsnips, and turnips, and breeding sheep. Madley's fortunes were furthered in 1382 when King Richard II allowed the village to hold a fair and market, which attracted trade from other villages. Fairs were used by travelling merchants to sell cloth and dressmaking products such as needles and thread, ribbons and buttons, and the markets provided an opportunity to sell farm produce such as eggs, butter, and wool. The village cross at Madley marks the site of the market.

When Henry VIII separated the Church of England from that of Rome, his most trusted friend and statesman, Sir Thomas More, refused to convert to Henry's new church. Henry had Thomas imprisoned and beheaded in Westminster in 1635. In fear of their own lives, Thomas' family fled to Madley where they lived in hiding. The refusal to submit to authority and attend Church of England services became known as Recusancy, and the prosecution and persecution of recusants lasted for over 100 years. Roman Catholics were particularly targeted, but anyone refusing to obey

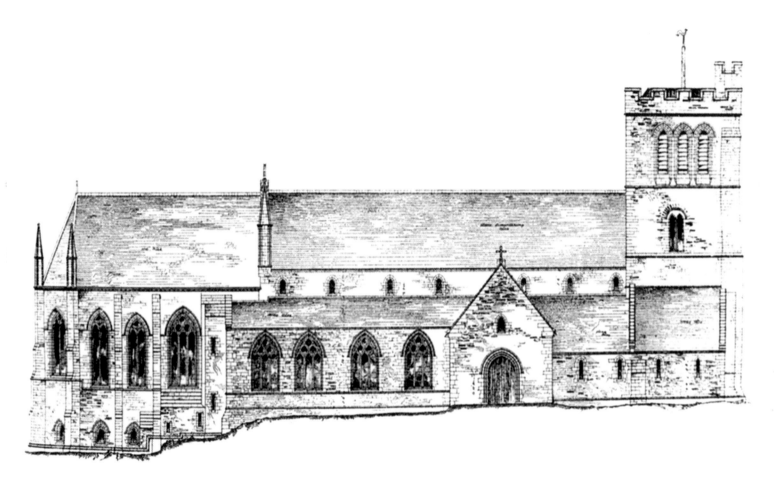

The north elevation of Madley church.
On the left is the chancel built c.1320 and with a polygonal apse, which is rare in Britain. The north porch is the oldest part of the building, dating from 1050–1100. The tower still contains the original door and ironwork of c.1250

the monarchy's strict religious doctrine and general authority was liable to be charged and called to account. For some, religious freedoms and flouting authority was worth an altercation with the local lord or dean. The counties of Lancashire, Durham, Yorkshire along with Wales took the lead in recusancy, but Herefordshire, too, showed recusant tendencies. The Church demanded that prayer was the only activity permitted on the Sabbath, so when Mr. Roger Pigg of Madley played a musical instrument before the Sabbath evening prayer, he was in trouble. Other Madley recusants included Mr. William Foote who was brought to account when he reportedly said he would dance in Madley churchyard 'in contempt and derogation of the churchwarden', a charge he denied but went on to commit — which led to his excommunication. Madley's most colourful disrupter of the peace was a lady known as Susan Seabourne. Described as 'a scolder, miser, slanderer, disturber, and abuser of her neighbours', her crimes were many. She called the vicar a dog; cursed her own father, beat him and tied him to a bedpost; abused the women of Madley, calling them whores; scolded the vicar and his wife, and said 'the clerk keeps a whore at his father's house and that he was pulled off his cousin who was with his child'. Another woman named N. Gardiner was found guilty of slander, and for her public penance she had a white sheet placed upon her and was made to walk up and down the aisle of the church recanting what she had said. When she left the church she swore she would never return.

Religious tensions increased at the time of the Civil War, and in 1641 Parliament passed an order that encouraged the 'defacing, demolishing, and quite taking away of all images, altars, or tables turned altarwise, crucifixes, superstitious pictures, monuments, and relicts of idolatry, out of all Churches or Chapels'. The head of the market cross was partially damaged as a result. That of the churchyard cross was removed and hidden to ensure its safe keeping. Indeed it was kept so safe that its existence was forgotten, and it was not until 1916 that it was found and replaced.

Madley was intrinsically Royalist at the start of the Civil War, as was most of Herefordshire. Fortunately the county saw little direct military action, with the exception of Hereford. When General Leslie's Scottish army laid siege to Hereford in support of the Parliamentary cause, they created much consternation in an ever widening area as they searched for supplies. In reaction to both this and the increasing Royalist demands for manpower from its western recruiting base, the country folk became ever more neutral in their attitude, and likely to support the Clubmen who were a form of mutual self protection.

Parliament proved the stronger in the end, and once secure in power ordered that all church decoration be eliminated. The villagers of Madley hid the church's stained glass windows before Cromwell's men could destroy them, but the colourful church walls were painted plain white, and the medieval art work on the walls was hidden behind coats of limewash. Cromwell died in 1658, and after two years of political turmoil the monarchy was reinstated with King Charles II who was much more tolerant of religious freedoms. Indeed, the king was more open-minded about a lot of things. One of his mistresses was an actress called Nell Gwynne, who was reputedly born in Hereford. Gwynne Street, near Hereford Cathedral, is named after her.

Farming continued to be the main occupation in Madley. The area has long been associated with Ryeland sheep, and it is thought that the breed originated in the region. The breed is mentioned in references that date back to the 12th century. Ryeland sheep were best known for their wool. In the 16th century the finest garments were made from it, and it is reputed that Queen Elizabeth I was so impressed with a pair of Ryeland wool stockings which she was presented, that she insisted from then on wearing only garments made from Ryeland wool. During the 17th and 18th centuries the breed was cross-bred to produce an animal farmed for its mutton. By 1902 pure bred Ryeland sheep were endangered, with only 14 flocks in existence. Today, thanks to resurgence in interest of old and rare breeds, the Ryeland has made a good comeback. Hereford cattle are another success story of Herefordshire's farming history. First mentioned in texts dating to the 16th century, the red and white cattle are now a common sight across farming regions in USA, Australia, South America and Europe. The farms around Madley and the rest of the county were also great producers of apples and pears from which cider and perry was made. On the coronation of Queen Anne in 1702, an orchard of perry pears was planted in her honour. Most of the farms in Madley produced some apples or pears for their own home-made cider.

With the coming of the Industrial Revolution and depression in agriculture, people moved to the cities to find work. The population of Madley declined from 970 residents in 1861 to 723 residents in 1911. After the First World War the population reached a new low of 677 residents.

War comes to Madley

After the First World War, a lot of country customs and superstitions dwindled. Madley, however, was still a relatively isolated village despite the improvements of rail and road networks. It was not until 1919 that the first bus service to Hereford became operational, providing a twice weekly service to the city. Prior to this the only means of public transport available was offered by Betsy Alcock, who for a small fee would transport passengers or wares in a cart pulled by her donkey, Bill. Betsy was very fond of Bill, and allowed him to live in the house with her and eat at the table. But Betsy also had a temper, and if Bill had enraged her he only had bread for his meal. If she was really angry with him she would temporarily banish him from the house. One day Bill was misbehaving and she chased him outside, only for the poor donkey to fall down a nearby well. It took a team of local men using a makeshift system of pulleys and ropes to get Bill out, and once free he was immediately revived with a drink of elderberry wine.

Not all Madley residents were as quirky as Betsy, though some still continued the old country superstitions. To ensure good crops in the autumn, a ceremony would take place on the afternoon of Easter Sunday. Local farmers and their families would meet in the field or orchard to be blessed. They would enjoy plum cake and cider, then bury some cake in a corner of the field and pour cider on it in a belief that the offering would ensure a good harvest. In late summer, once the harvest was gathered in, it was customary to celebrate with a feast, and a sheaf of plaited wheat would be hung above the farmhouse door to bring the household good fortune in the coming year. Today, some practices may seem strange, even distasteful, such as the tradition of allowing a child to hold a pig's tail whilst it was being slaughtered. Such customs slowly disappeared as transport and communication links with the outside world expanded, and attitudes changed.

Madley village was also changing. The population slowly grew after the end of the First World War, and various clubs and organisations were formed to provide entertainment and opportunities to socialise. In 1919 the Girl Guides formed a group in Madley, and a year later Madley Tennis Club started and was such a success that a pavilion was built in 1926. The Madley branch of the Women's Institute (WI) began in 1923, and from 1932 until the outbreak of war they organised an annual Christmas party for the village. The WI was an integral part of village life; they raised money for the Red Cross and other charities; sent eggs and money to Hereford hospitals; and organised day trips for Madley residents.

The new bus link to and from Hereford proved popular, and some locals travelled so regularly into the city that drivers would wait if they were not at the bus stop on time. The bus would also detour to collect regular customers, and would drop them back at their door in the afternoon. Hereford had everything the discerning Madley resident could want: furs from Edwards in High Town, hats from King & Sons in Commercial Road, and Greenlands department store in High Town even had a toy department for the children, and its carpeted arcades were considered rather posh. A trip into Hereford also provided a chance to enjoy a film at the Odeon cinema, a favourite entertainment of adults and children alike. The cinema screened newsreels as well as feature films. In the 1930s the threat of war was drawing closer, and the newsreels played a major role in keeping the public informed. On Sunday 3 September 1939 the news broadcast a speech by the Prime Minister, Neville Chamberlain. In it he announced that Britain was indeed at war with Germany. Within hours, preparations for war were under way in Herefordshire. Army personnel knocked on doors to ascertain which private houses in the area had room to billet one or two servicemen, and air raid sirens were tested. People thought that German planes would be overhead dropping bombs almost immediately, but it was to be some time before the first Luftwaffe aircraft was spotted over Herefordshire. The Prime Minister's announcement created an initial flurry of activity and rationing of some products, but Madley and Herefordshire soon settled back into normal daily routine. It was not until the Battle of Britain that the county was really affected by the war.

The Battle of Britain began in July 1940 when Hitler ordered his Luftwaffe air force to conduct reconnaissance flights over England to establish the locations of the RAF bases and airfields. Hitler wanted to invade Britain, but to land his troops by sea would prove too dangerous if the RAF could defend the English coast from the air. Hitler needed to destroy the RAF, and he was so confident that his air force would accomplish this he ordered German troops to assemble along the French coast to wait to be transported across the Channel. The Luftwaffe conducted wave after wave of bombing missions over south-east England with the aim of destroying all RAF aircraft and airfields. The missions proved effective, and the RAF suffered many losses of both personnel and aircraft. Ground crew and mechanics took heavy casualties as they worked in broad daylight on open airfields to repair runways and aircraft. Spare parts became scarce. The RAF was buckling under the pressure of constant attacks. The Luftwaffe stepped up the bombardment, and introduced night flying ensuring the RAF had no reprieve from the constant bombing. Hitler had instructed that civilian towns were not to be targeted. He knew any action against civilians would create a very hostile population which would be harder to indoctrinate into Nazi ideology once he had successfully completed his invasion of Britain. However, on 24 August one Luftwaffe raid that was intended for military targets near London, drifted off course and hit the capital. The following day the battered RAF gathered a force and mounted a mission against Berlin, and bombed the city, doing so again three days later and for a third time two days after that. Hitler was furious that Germany's capital had been attacked by such a weakened RAF. His tactics changed from targeting military airfields and aircraft to openly attacking civilian towns, cities, factories and industry. From 7 September London was bombed for 57 consecutive nights. The Blitz raids on the civilian targets allowed the RAF time to regroup, repair aircraft and runways, and launch a head on attack on the Luftwaffe's planes. To combat the German night raids the RAF installed radar in their aircraft. This allowed them to locate the Luftwaffe aircraft and intercept them before they dropped their bombs on British towns. RAF pilots and air crew, whose numbers were greatly reduced due to the heavy losses they had already suffered, were pushed to the maximum. Personnel flew missions around the clock with very little time for sleep. Just as the RAF crews were becoming exhausted by the constant strain, Hitler changed his tactics again. He diverted his attention to attacking Russia, and Britain's constant bombardment from the Luftwaffe subsided.

The Battle of Britain affected Madley in two ways. The blitz bombing of British towns and cities instigated a wave of evacuations from urban areas into the countryside, children from Liverpool and London coming to Madley to be away from the Luftwaffe's bombs. Many had never been to the country before, and whilst some found the sudden relocation exciting, for others it was a dreadful experience. Evacuated children arriving in the county would first be taken to Hereford Cattle Market where it was decided which village they would be sent to. They were then handed over to the families with whom they were to live. Some of the city children were surprised by what they found in the country — the earth was reddy-brown, not black as it was in the industrial towns, and the air smelt different. Most city children were used to indoor bathrooms with hot and cold running water, but Madley homes usually had an outside toilet and often no running water in the house at all. Water would have to be collected from a well, or by using a hand pump. Evacuee children were also used to electric light and electric cookers, but in Madley there was no electricity, and households were lit by oil lamps, and cooking was done on oil stoves or in ovens built into fireplaces. Fires were also used to heat irons to press clothing. The lack of modern amenities was a shock to many children, but the worst thing about Madley was the lack of a fish and chip shop. Indeed, food generally was different — a lot had to be picked and harvested, rather than bought at a shop. There were no electric fridges, and consequently a lot of food was salted, pickled, dried or bottled. Meat was usually from an animal that had been butchered on the premises, then stored on a cold slab in the pantry. Some children did not adjust to this rustic and old fashioned way of life, preferring instead to risk the German bombs, and returned to the cities. Those who stayed could enjoy the freedom of the picturesque Herefordshire countryside. But even the quiet countryside did not always avoid the attacks aimed at the cities. In 1940 the blitz was raining down on Liverpool. The Luftwaffe bombers would fly from their bases in occupied France and use the reflection of the moon on the sea and the main rivers as a guide to their destination target. Sometimes returning German planes would use the Wye as their guide, dropping any remaining bombs en route. One such random bombing occurred at Kingstone, just a couple of miles from Madley.

The tremendous losses suffered by the RAF during the Battle of Britain meant that it needed to regain its strength of numbers as quickly as possible. The service had to recruit and train as many pilots, air crew and ground crew as was possible, for which new training facilities had also to be established. The airfields that were operational at the time were needed to conduct sorties and bombing raids over Germany, and therefore could not be used. It was also vital that any new training bases be located away from the threat of German bombers that haunted the east and south of the country. The result was the procurement of sites in the West Country and South Wales, to reserve eastern air space for active service missions. Herefordshire is the geographical boundary between the midland plains in the east, and the highlands of Wales to the west. Potential sites any further west would encounter the Black Mountains and Radnorshire mountains, both dangerous obstacles for young pilots. Madley has hills on three sides which provided some protection from enemy aircraft but were relatively

TELEPHONE: HOLBORN 3434
Extn. 1232.

Any communications on the
subject of this letter should
be addressed to :—
THE
UNDER SECRETARY
OF STATE, AIR MINISTRY,
and the following number
quoted :—

A.120401/40.W.6.(b).

AIR MINISTRY, DEPT.H.O.,
LONDON, W.C.2.

1st October, 1940.

Sir,

MADLEY, HEREFORD.

I am directed to acknowledge the receipt of
your letter of the 29th ultimo, and in reply I am to say
that the Air Ministry have decided to adopt the site at
Madley for an aerodrome, and I am to ask you to inform
your tenant accordingly.

I am, Sir,

Your obedient Servant,

for Director of Works.

Donald Parsons Esq.,
    Street House,
        Madley,
            Hereford.

A.120389/40/W.6.(b).

AIR MINISTRY, (Dept. HO.)
LONDON, W.C.2.

28th October, 1940.

Sir,

Land or premises at Madley.

I am directed to refer to previous correspondence
and/or interviews on the above matter and to inform you that at the
present time the Air Ministry can only take up land under the powers
conferred by the Defence Regulations, 1939.

In lieu, therefore, of the normal peace-time procedure
of serving Notice to Treat, it is necessary to requisition your
property under the Regulations and the Form of Requisition is
forwarded herewith, in duplicate. One copy, with the receipt
signed, should be returned in the enclosed envelope.

A supply of Claim Form 1 is also enclosed for completion
and return in due course, in duplicate.

Before any work is done on the property the Lands
Officer responsible for taking possession will visit the site and
discuss detailed arrangements with the occupier. Subject to
essential Air Ministry requirements, every facility will be given to
enable the occupier to harvest and remove his produce and to remove
his stock.

I am to add that procedure under the Regulations will not
preclude sale and purchase by agreement if the Air Ministry decide that
that property is required for permanent retention.

I am, Sir,
Your obedient Servant,

for Director of Works.

Mr. Parsons,
    Street House,
        Madley,
            Hereford.

C.20007.

*This page and opposite: some of the correspondence that flowed
in quick succession to allow the Air Ministry to take over the
necessary land and start construction of RAF Madley*

A.120401/40/W.6.b.   A.M. FORM 1553.

An Agreement made the 9th day of January

1941 BETWEEN Mr. Donald Parsons

of Street House Farm, Madley, Herefordshire,

of the one part and THE SECRETARY OF STATE FOR AIR

(hereinafter called " the Department ") of the other part.

*Insert description of the property.

WHEREAS the Department has taken possession of* Three pieces of Pasture and Arable land O.S. Nos. 18, 23, and 707, and part 14, containing 27.085 acres situate at Madley in the County of Herefordshire as from the 1st 4th day of November October, 1940.

pursuant to the powers conferred on it by the Defence Regulations

1939 by reason of which compensation is or will be payable to the

said Mr. Donald Parsons

under the provisions of the Compensation (Defence) Act 1939.

It is hereby agreed between the parties hereto that the Department

shall pay and the said Mr. Donald Parsons

shall accept payment at the rate of £ 80 (Eighty Pounds)

per annum payable quarterly on the usual quarter days in satis-

faction of the sums which may be payable pursuant to Section

2 (1) (a) and of interest thereon under Section 10 of the said Act. The said compensation shall be payable as from and including the 1st 4th day of November October, 1940.

AS WITNESS the hands of the parties hereto.

Witness to the signature of Mr. Donald Parsons.

Edith C. Hames.
Street House Madley

Witness to the signature of
R. J. HODDELL,
on behalf of the SECRETARY OF STATE FOR AIR
Gordon Dick.
Air Ministry.

---

low, so would not unduly endanger trainee RAF pilots. Therefore it could be said that Madley was the most westerly location that was a suitable site for an aerodrome.

Once Madley had been chosen, the Air Ministry had to procure all land and dwellings that were occupying the Stoney Street site. In October 1940 the Air Ministry contacted the owner of Street House Farm, Mr. Donald Parsons, who ran a poultry business, notifying him that 'it is necessary to requisition your property under the Regulations and the Form of Requisition is forwarded herewith'. The farm consisted of a Georgian style farmhouse, a cider house with granary, stables, barns, poultry houses, pig sty, trap house, and coach house. Mr. Parsons was paid £80 per year for the use of his poultry farm. Mr. Edge at Parkway sold his land to the Ministry and a hangar was built near his old farmhouse. Once all the required land was obtained, construction of the new base began. Towards the end of 1940 contractors were on site to clear trees and hedges, and dispose of any remaining farming equipment, including a hayrick. When cleared, they started laying the perimeter track, and the building work began in earnest.

The base was essentially constructed in a little over six months, and in July 1941 a small group of servicemen arrived to prepare the station for use. During the construction, the base had been under the control of No 27 Group, Flying Training Command, but on 27 August 1941 RAF Madley No 4 Radio School was officially formed, under the command of Flight Lieutenant P.F.W. Pictor-Wayneric, who was also commander of nearby RAF Credenhill. However, there were still no accommodation or messing facilities for either officers or airmen, and the few personnel had to be billeted some miles away at RAF Credenhill. On 17 September

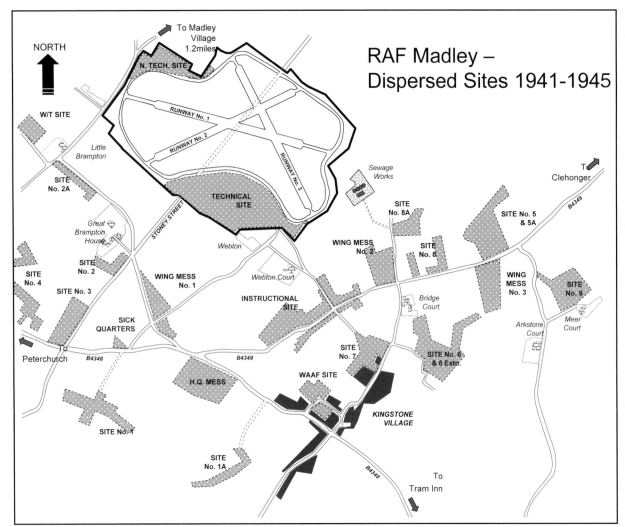

RAF Madley –
Dispersed Sites 1941-1945

NORTH

To Madley Village 1.2miles

N. TECH. SITE

W/T SITE

Little Brampton

RUNWAY No. 1

RUNWAY No. 2

RUNWAY No. 3

SITE No. 2A

Great Brampton House

SITE No. 2

TECHNICAL SITE

STONEY STREET

Webton

Sewage Works

SITE No. 8A

To Clehonger

B4349

SITE No. 5 & 5A

WING MESS No. 2

SITE No. 8

SITE No. 4

SITE No. 3

WING MESS No. 1

Webton Court

WING MESS No. 3

SITE No. 9

SICK QUARTERS

INSTRUCTIONAL SITE

Bridge Court

Arkstone Court

Meer Court

To Peterchurch

B4348

B4349

SITE No. 7

SITE No. 6 & 6 Extn.

H.Q. MESS

WAAF SITE

KINGSTONE VILLAGE

SITE No. 1

SITE No. 1A

B4348

To Tram Inn

Site Buildings

All sites had latrine blocks, air raid shelters, picket posts and rain water storage tanks, In addition:

Sick Quarters Site
Sick quarters & annexe
Ambulance garage & mortuary
Barrack block

Headquarters Post
Institute
Officers Mess
Sergeants Mess
Dining Room
Squash Court
Sergeants & Civilian Instructors showers
Grocery & local produce store
NAAFI staff quarters
Central Station store
Tailors, Shoemakers & barber Shop
Medical Inspection & Dental Block
Airmens ablutions & showers
Gymnasium with church annexe
Fuel Compound
WAAF camp & Ablutions
Officers Bath House
Cinema

WAAF Site
Sergeants Mess, Dining Room & Institute
Officers Mess & quarters
Sick quarters
Decontam Centre J type
barrack Hut
Fuel Compound
WAAF Institute
WAAF Ablutions & hairdressing ext.

Instructional Site
Common Rooms
Visual Instruction Signalling Block
Morse, Technical, General Education,
Air Operations etc. Classrooms and Labs
Examination Hall & Library
School Headquarters
Trade Test Board
Oil Store
Harwell Boxes
Sub Station incoming
Stand by Set House
Dispersed Site Transformer, Distribution Centre
& Battery Charging Room
Fuel Compound
Armament Training Block
Stores
Night Vision Testing Room

No 1 Wing Mess Site
(similar to other Wings' Mess Sites)
Institute
Dining Room
Wing Offices
Squadron Offices
Wing Store
Ration Store
Airmens Showers
Decontam Centre M type
Fuel Store
Medical Inspection Hut
WAAF camp & Ablutions

Site No 1
Officers, W/O, Sergeants and Airmens Quarters
Ablution Blocks
Subsidiary Fuel Compound

Other sites consisted of differing mixes of
quarters and associated ablution etc. blocks

Aerial photograph of 1946 looking south over the runways to the technical site

15

1941 command passed to Group Captain T. Fagan. On 2 October 1941 a small group of 68 airmen transferred to Madley for Guard Duty, the Guard Room and the completed HQ offices being used as billets. The airmen still had no messing facilities, and had to be fed by the canteen used by the workers from the construction firm Mowlem who were building the base. Five days later, on 7 October 1941, the balance of the airmen who had been billeted at RAF Credenhill transferred to RAF Madley, although officers who were not able to secure billets in the village had to remain based at RAF Credenhill until the officers' quarters were completed. It was not until 28 November 1941 that RAF Madley became truly operational with the arrival of the first allocation of 72 trainees. Just two weeks later, on 12 December 1941, the order was given to suspend any further intake of trainees due to the delay completing the domestic sites. Once the base was fully operational the local population rose from the 292 residents, as quoted by the 1931 census, to approximately 5,000 people.

The RAF had learnt from its experiences in the Battle of Britain that it was sensible to maintain a low density for both personnel and aircraft, so the base was dispersed over a large area. Indeed RAF Madley proved to be one of the largest training bases in the country, being spread over 3½ square miles. The site was divided into 21 separate areas from Batcho Hill on the Peterchurch Road, to Great Brampton House on the west; and to the east, Meer Court and Arkstone Court. The base covered an area from Henley Court to Gooses Foot, Whitehouse Farm, Bridge Court, and Turners House to the south of the Hereford road. It also incorporated part of Kingstone School grounds, which still show evidence of the First Aid Post and a nearby air-raid shelter. Bomb shelters were made of reinforced concrete up to 2 metres thick, and had a steel escape hatch in the roof. They were covered with soil, and had internal blast doors. The shelters weighed so much they had to be transported and constructed in sections. Transportation of materials and workers was a logistical problem for Mowlem, who had secured the building contract, in particular for the Clerk of Works, Mr. John Houston. Each morning, seven days a week, 36 busloads of employees were transported to the site to work from 7am until 6pm. Hardcore was delivered by train to Vowchurch station a few miles away. Local people and farmers were hired as drivers, and used farm tractors and trailers to transport the thousands of tons of hardcore from the station to the site. Stone for the construction of buildings was transported by road from the Forest of Dean, and had to be unloaded by hand. Mowlem employees were paid 5s. 6d. (28p) per hour for the heavy work they did, often in terrible weather conditions. A power plant was built to generate electricity to provide light and power to all areas of the site, and a drainage system installed to remove excessive surface water from the three proposed runways, along with a sewerage farm. A well was sunk near Eaton Bishop from where water was pumped, and stored in a 100,000 gallon tank in woodland half a mile from the HQ mess site.

The runways were built over an old strawberry farm in a layout based on those of RAF Millom in Cumbria. The grass runways ran in three directions — east to west, south-west to north-east, and north-west to south-east — to allow for a variety of take off and landing options, according to the direction of the wind. They measured 1,100 yards x 100 yards, 1,100 yards x 70 yards and 1,400 yards x 380 yards respectively. In October 1943 the grass runways were reinforced with an airstrip of Sommerfeld tracking made from prefabricated 5 metre square concrete slabs overlaid with tarmac. In the southern part of the site two Callender Hamilton hangars and three Hinaidi hangars were located. The latter were a 1920s design and had a high roof with external gantries either side of the sliding doors. When the doors were slid open they were supported by the metal arm, so allowing the doors to be pushed beyond the dimensions of the actual building. This allowed the hangars to accommodate a complete aircraft, wings and all. The hangars were 35 metres long and made from a prefabricated steel matrix encased in corrugated asbestos sheeting. The floors were concrete. Hinaidi hangars were initially used as classrooms and the Callender Hamilton hangars used to house aircraft, but as the number of aircraft on the base increased and the instructional block was completed, all hangars were given over to aircraft. A few years later two further Callender Hamilton hangars were added to the north of the site, and in December 1942 work commenced on the 13 Blister hangars that were dispersed around the perimeter. This gave the base the capacity to have up to 60 Proctor aircraft, 18 Dominie aircraft and 100 Gypsy engines. Sometimes other aircraft came to RAF Madley, and it saw Oxfords, Magisters, Hurricanes, Masters, Tigermoths, and Spitfires.

From July 1941 to January 1943 the station was also used by No 8 Anti Aircraft Co-operation Unit with their Lysander, Oxford, and Blenheim aircraft, based at Pembridge and later split between Shobdon and Madley. They looked after all the Anti Aircraft gun sites and searchlight stations in the surrounding countryside, dividing their time between Madley and RAF Shobdon. Sometimes RAF Madley would also house Tomahawks and Mustangs for short periods whilst they were on Army exercises. One local resident, Mr. Ernest Griffiths, who was a boy when the base was operational, remembers the wing of a parked training aircraft protruding over their garden hedge.

Overleaf is a table of the aircraft stationed at RAF Madley from 1941 to 1946. Figures obtained from RAF Madley Operational Diaries, National Archives, Kew.

The base had to accommodate a large permanent staff as well as the cadets of the Radio School. There were eight accommodation sites spread about for officers, NCOs and airmen. There was also a self contained site for WAAF personnel, including messing and accommodation for all ranks. The RAF commanders thought ahead when planning the site, and the servicemen's accommodation was located far away from the WAAFs to stop any unauthorised after hours fraternising. Even so, one WAAF remembers that, when sharing a Nissen hut with a friend, one evening as they were removing their curlers in preparation for going out, they saw a face at the window — a peeping Tom! RAF airmen who were married sometimes moved their wives

Hinaidi hangar top, and Callender Hamilton below

Date	Dominies	Proctors	Oxfords	Magisters	Hurricanes	Master	Tigermoth	Spitfire	Total
December 1941	8	11							19
January 1942	10	22	1						33
February 1942	10	34	1						45
March 1942	16	45	1						62
April & May 1942	18	57							75
June 1942	18	58							76
July 1942	17	48		2					67
August & September 1942	18	61		2					81
October 1942	18	67	1						86
November 1942	18	71		2					91
December 1942	18	67		2					87
January to March 1943	18	77		2					97
April 1943	18	76	1	2					97
May 1943	18	77	1	2					98
June & July 1943	18	75	1	2					96
August 1943	18	77	1	2					98
September 1943	18	76	1	2					97
October 1943	17	84	1	2					104
November 1943	17	74	1	2					94
December 1943 & January 1944	18	73	1	2					94
February 1944	18	84	1	2					105
March 1944	18	85	1	2	1	1			108
April 1944	18	82	1	2	2	1			106
May 1944	18	70	1	2	2	1			94
June 1944	18	81	1	2	2	1			105
July 1944	18	100	1	2		1			122
August 1944	18	90	1	2		1	2		114
September 1944	17	91	1	1		1	2		113
October 1944	18	87	1	1	1	1	2		111
November 1944	18	91	1	1	1	1	2		115
December 1944	16	91	1	1	1	1	2		113
January 1945	18	84	1	2	1	2	2		110
February 1945	18	90	1	2	1	1	2		115
March 1945	20	88	1	2	1	1	2		115
April 1945	19	84	1	2	1	1	2		110
May 1945	19	84	1	1	1		2		108
June 1945	19	82	2	2	1		2	1	109
July 1945	15	75	2		1		2	2	97
August 1945	15	77	2		1		2	1	98
September 1945	15	77	1		1		2		96
October 1945	14	75	2		1		2		94
November 1945	14	70	2		1		2		89
December 1945	11	71	2		1		2		87
January 1946	8	47	2		1		2		60
February 1946	8	46	1				2		57
March 1946	7	43	1				2		53
April 1946	6	38	1				2		47
May 1946	6	33	1				2		42
June 1946	6	33	1				2		42
July–Oct 1946	5	33	1				2		41

Table of the aircraft stationed at RAF Madley from 1941 to 1946. (Figures obtained from RAF Madley Operational Diaries, National Archives) and families into the area, to be billed in private houses in Madley village. One such wife billed nearby was author Catherine Cookson, whose husband Tom was stationed at RAF Madley. The Stinton family with whom she lodged had a small boy called John, and Catherine wrote one of her earliest stories for him called *Stinton Got His Man* which was a tale about a Canadian Mountie, also called John.

Accommodation on the base itself for the servicemen and servicewomen was in very basic Nissen huts, which, with their rounded corrugated iron roofs, provided little comfort, tending to be sweltering in summer and freezing in winter. Cadets stationed at the base remember the beds being extremely hard, with one blanket underneath and other blankets on top that were so rough they would scratch so much it was hard to sleep. Some cadets resorted to folding newspaper around their neck to stop their skin being rubbed raw. The huts had no electric light, so hurricane lamps or tilley lamps were used. The huts also did not have a sewerage system, so personnel would have to use buckets at night as the latrines and ablution blocks were far away, near the mess sites. The men's Nissen huts were located near woods, which was handy for gathering wood for the stoves. Each hut had at least one stove, but there was never enough fuel to keep them burning brightly. When fuel ran out there was no option but to raid the supplies of any hut that had recently received a fuel delivery. Even furniture and fences were used to keep the home fires burning. The stoves were also the cause of the very high rate of misdemeanours on the base. Offenders who broke the rules could expect three to seven days confined to barracks as punishment. This meant reporting to the guardroom after the evening meal, and being put on fatigues in the cookhouse. However, the extra duties in the cookhouse provided the ideal opportunity to pilfer items that were usually rationed. Butter and fat for cooking, eggs, bacon, and bread, in fact all the ingredients for a good old fry up on their Nissen hut stove could be acquired whilst on cookhouse fatigues. But the stoves also proved a source of misery, as they did not provide sufficient warmth for the occupants in winter. One WAAF veteran remembers sharing a Nissen hut with two other WAAF friends. It was a bitter winter and being rationed to one bucket of coal per day, their stove had run out of fuel. They burnt everything they could spare in an effort to keep warm. Then one of her friends, a newly-wed bride remembered she had her husband's love letters. In a desperate attempt to warm their freezing hut she burnt all of them. The flames lasted just a fleeting moment and offered very little warmth. Three days later she received news that her husband had been killed in action.

Personnel on the base were divided into four Wings: one was for air crew, two for ground crew and there was one HQ Wing. Each Wing had its own mess site, as did the WAAF personnel. Cadets were marched to and from the mess site every meal-time; sometimes they could cover several miles a day if their lessons took place in the far corners of the aerodrome. They had to carry everything in their knapsack: mugs, plates, knives, forks, radio equipment and books, P.T. gear, flying boots as well as carry a rifle. The endless trudging around the base resulted in the unofficial motto 'Never have so many walked so far'! One cadet calculated that during his stay at RAF Madley he marched 1,200 miles!

The mess conversations were a quick induction to life in general for some young personnel. One veteran who was only 17 when he was stationed at RAF Madley remembers the Sergeants' mess was quite an eye opener for a young lad. Opposite the mess was a large open tank where cadets had to wash their eating irons (knife, fork and spoon). It was supposed to contain hot water, but was usually luke warm and greasy after several hundred airmen had used it.

HQ Wing and its mess site were located near the road to Hay-on-Wye. The technical, administrative and instructional buildings were located to the south of the base. The Instructional site was on the road from Coldwell to Coldstone Cross and Dews Corner, which meant it was near the perimeter of the base. Behind the Instructional site was a civilian enterprise, Hartley's Jam Factory. The factory was sometimes short of staff, and the C.O. gave permission for a few cadets to work there in their own time. Cadets helped to move large barrels of fruit, and stack jam jars in cases. Some cadets even cycled to Ross-on-Wye to pick apples and cherries. They were paid either a shilling or two pocket money, or given a quantity of sugar, which was a treat as it was so scarce due to rationing. In summer the air surrounding the factory was always buzzing with wasps which made patrolling that area of the site a little less comfortable. The station's Sick Quarters, located on a corner of Stoney Street fronting onto the Peterchurch Road, dealt with any stings. There was also a fully equipped hospital on site which had two wards of 50 beds each, two isolation wards, an operating theatre, dispensary, ambulance service and kitchen facilities. The hospital was needed for accidents, casualties of crashes, and the sufferers of stomach bugs that sometimes occurred on a large scale. In 1943, gastro problems occurred which may have been linked to a bad batch of minced meat, and many personnel suffered as a result.

On another occasion Mr. W. Owen remembers the speed of medical treatment. One morning he reported to the duty doctor at 0800 hours. He was sent on to the station's Sick Quarters, then was transferred to RAF Credenhill hospital and his appendix was removed by noon. Mr. Peter Brewster did not receive such swift attention, however. Due to a contagious illness he was confined to barracks and the only person allowed in was the Medical Officer. Even his meals were left outside on a tray on the ground. Dental treatment was also slow to be provided on base. It was not until 1944 that construction of a dental centre began, and it took until May 1945 for the station to gain a Dental Officer.

The Examination Hall and Library were housed in Building 27, which measured 10 metres by 36 metres, of brick construction with concrete cladding and a corrugated asbestos roof. The building was visible from Kingstone School, and training cadets and schoolchildren could sympathize with each other at exam time. Like the local schoolchildren, the cadets' lessons took place in classrooms which were located all over the site. When walking from one class to another in winter they were protected from the elements by a ground sheet that would be worn over the shoulders and hang down to their knees; the water would run down the surface and drench the cadets' lower legs and feet. One cadet, Mr. Stimson, remembers that the trainees were marched in columns of three to classes along the roads. Their leader would walk half way along the columns, in the middle of the road. Petrol rationing ensured there were few or no vehicles to disrupt his orderly march. In winter, if there were no blackout restrictions, a white light would be carried in front of the men and a red light behind as a safety precaution. The station also had many facilities for personnel to relax and spend their free time. These included a cinema, squash court, gymnasium, church, grocery and produce store, tailor, shoemaker, barber, and NAAFI which contained a snooker table.

Life at RAF Madley

RAF Madley was established to train 2,800 Wireless Operators (Ground crew) and 1,200 Wireless Operators (Air crew). Cadets had to complete the Ground crew part of the training first before they were promoted to the Air crew course. New arrivals on the base would be given a note from the Commander-in-Chief which set out the objectives of the station and the role each individual must play if Britain was to win the war. Below is a transcript:

> The object of all our training is to give you skill and confidence to perform any task which may be allotted to you.
>
> You must train yourself to think quickly and accurately and act with vigour and resolution; you must furbish your mind and toughen your body. You must be keen and alert at all times, always thinking about and living in your job. You must cultivate a thirst for knowledge, the kind which enables you to perform your task most effectively and to help others, too, to be most effective. You must ensure that all your gear is in first-class condition. Nothing less is good enough.
>
> There is no room for slackness or inefficiency, for upon your efficiency depends not only your own safety but that of others.
>
> You are up against a ruthless barbarian enemy, whether german or japanese, who has no code of honour or sportsmanship. He is a trained and capable killer in perfect condition, who must be beaten in his own style. There is no room for half measures or any slacking off after your earlier training is over. You must always keep yourself up to date and in first rate condition mentally and physically.
>
> Remember then that in order to play our part in this war we must have a burning keenness backed by essential knowledge, good discipline and a defiant spirit. Never forget, however, that in addition to your task of becoming a cool, efficient aggressive fighter you also have great responsibilities whether as an officer or N.C.O. in looking after your men, without whose efforts the success of the R.A.F. would not be possible. Their share in any success you may attain is probably far greater than you readily imagine, so see to it that they do receive from you full credit for their work. Your appreciation can best be shown by looking after their interests in every way and by good airmanship eliminating all the unnecessary work which results from thoughtless handling.
>
> P. Babington
> Air Marshal, Commanding-in-Chief, Flying Training Command

By the end of December 1941, according to the station's operational diaries, RAF Madley was home to 41 officers, 1,375 airmen and staff, 72 trainee ground crew cadets, and 1 member of the Women's Auxiliary Air Force (WAAF). During December the station had received deliveries of fire appliances, technical equipment for radios and transmitters, a supply of aviation fuel, and racks to accommodate the anti-gas equipment which would become frequently used in drills and exercises. Eight Dominie aircraft and 11 Proctors were also received in December ready for the cadets to begin their training.

On arrival at the base, new recruits were fed by the Women's Volunteer Service who supplied beetroot or onion sandwiches and mugs of hot tea. A cadet spent his first day on base checking in, filling out forms, being shown to his Nissen hut and around the other facilities on the base. Cadets were also issued with their kit,

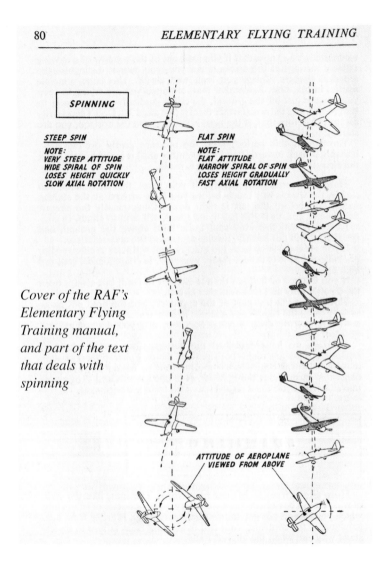

SPINNING

STEEP SPIN

NOTE:
VERY STEEP ATTITUDE
WIDE SPIRAL OF SPIN
LOSES HEIGHT QUICKLY
SLOW AXIAL ROTATION

FLAT SPIN

NOTE:
FLAT ATTITUDE
NARROW SPIRAL OF SPIN
LOSES HEIGHT GRADUALLY
FAST AXIAL ROTATION

**ATTITUDE OF AEROPLANE
VIEWED FROM ABOVE**

Cover of the RAF's Elementary Flying Training manual, and part of the text that deals with spinning although items of clothing and bedding were often scarce, and they had to make do with whatever was available. On 30 October 1942, the poor state of the cadets' kit prompted a parade to show Squadron Leader Jackson the extent of the problem.

On the second day cadets were introduced to Morse code, and they conducted some drill, but the majority of the time was still spent organising. The third day saw their training start in earnest. One cadet, Mr. Edgar Turner, remembers how a typical day began for the new recruits to the Ground Crew Wireless/ Telegraphy Operator course. 'We were up at 0600 hours to walk to the Community Centre for a wash and shave, generally in cold water! Then into the Cookhouse for bacon or sausage or spam with beans and the inevitable potatoes, generally mashed, and tea by the gallons! We were assembled into squads at 0730 hours and marched to the respective area for tuition.' Daily classes usually began at 0800 hours, and concluded at 1700 hours Monday to Friday, and sometimes also Saturdays. Extra classes and duties were also conducted in the evenings, leaving a new cadet little time to himself. Sundays were free, but personnel were encouraged to attend the church parade at 1000 hours. One cadet remembers that on his fourth day at the base he attended the church parade but, as the rest of the day was free he walked into Madley village, where he discovered to his joy there were 'two houses – and both of them public!' The church held regular services for personnel, and sometimes would also hold a special service to mark a particular occasion. Every September a National Day of Prayer was held, and on 28 April 1943 a service celebrated the 25th anniversary of the formation of the RAF.

In January 1942 the accommodation sites were still not complete, and recruit intake continued to be suspended, but the base had received 300 metal bunks beds, as well as more training equipment and wireless transmitters. The weather in early 1942 was extremely bad. Heavy snow hampered the completion of the building, and bad visibility effectively grounded all aircraft. But by February 1942 the weather eased, and some flying had been achieved, with 233.55 flying hours recorded in the Operational Diaries. The station also received refuelling trailers to be used on the airfield. On 19 February the station was able to resume the intake of cadets. A further intake occurred on 26 February and, from then until 1946 RAF Madley received a regular intake of cadet wireless operators. (See appendices A and B for intake and passing out numbers for both Air and Ground cadets). Ground crew cadets were usually sent to RAF Madley after completing initial training at RAF Yatesbury or Blackpool, but a few arrived from other parts of the country. On 19 March RAF Madley received the first intake of Air crew cadets, many of whom came from Bournemouth.

In the early days of the base the standard Ground crew cadet course lasted for 16 weeks, although later this was shortened as demand for trained personnel increased. Mr. Edgar Turner remembers 'we had practice in sending and receiving Morse code. The instructor would send blocks of four letters in Morse, some quickly, some slowly. It was essential that we learnt sending and receiving Morse, as the pass out level was a minimum of 18 words per minute.' The Morse was transmitted to the cadet's headphones via a Creed machine which used perforated tape to indicate the dits and dahs (dots and dashes). If the corporal in charge of the lesson wanted a break from manually tapping the Morse himself, he could set the speed of the Creed machine, and Morse would transmit until the tape ran out. Pupils had to translate the Morse on the tape, which was either in plain language or in Syko, a group of four

AIR PUBLICATION 1762
Issued October, 1939

AIR MINISTRY

ELECTRICAL AND RADIO NOTES FOR WIRELESS OPERATORS

LONDON
HIS MAJESTY'S STATIONERY OFFICE
Price 3s. 6d. net

Cover of and a page from the manual used by cadets at RAF Madley, together with (opposite) the log that had to be completed after each flight and ratified by the training instructor

24

This also carries a pointer and a piston swinging within an air dash-pot, giving pneumatic damping. Spring or gravity control may be used.

The repulsion type has a short solenoid in which are placed two parallel soft-iron strips. One is fixed and the other is attached to a pointer. When current flows, both irons become similarly magnetised and move apart against the action of a spring. Both scale-shapes are non-uniform.

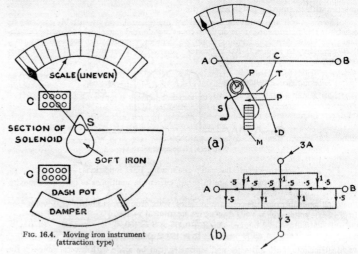

Fig. 16.4. Moving iron instrument (attraction type)

Fig. 17.4. Hot wire instrument

Hot wire instruments

Current passing in a wire generates heat which in its turn causes the wire to expand; this principle is employed to measure current in this type of instrument.

AB [fig. 17.4 (a)] is a fine wire through which the current to be measured passes. A phosphor-bronze wire CD is fixed to the centre of AB and anchored to the frame of the instrument at D; at the middle of CD is attached a silk thread T, which passes round a light grooved pulley P, and is fixed to a spring S. The pulley, which rests in jewelled bearings, also carries the needle of the instrument. As AB is heated by the current, it expands and sags; the spring S then takes up the slack in CD by pulling on the silk thread thus turning the pulley and moving the needle. Also attached to the pulley is a thin sheet of aluminium P, which, moving between the poles of a permanent magnet M, provides the necessary damping.

WIRELESS OPERATORS (AIR) LOG

SQUADRON *	AIRCRAFT		DATE	
CAPTAIN	NAVIGATOR		WIRELESS OP.	
AIRBORNE	NATURE OF FLIGHT *		LANDED	

N.F.T. (OR D.I.)			AFTER FLIGHT CHECK		
ITEM	S. OR U/S	INITIALS	ITEM	S OR U/S	INITIALS
INTER COMM.			INTER COMM.	OFF	
W/T TRANSMITTER			W/T TRANSMITTER	OFF	
W/T RECEIVER			W/T RECEIVER	OFF	
R/T SET			R/T SET	OFF	
I.F.F.			I.F.F.	OFF	
W/T SPARES			W/T SPARES		

CAPTAINS REMARKS (AFTER FLIGHT)			
J.D.A	R/T	INTER. COMM.	SIGNATURE

INFORMATION	
OPERATIONAL CALL SIGN:	STATION R/T AIRCRAFT CALL SIGN:
BASE COLLECTIVE CALL SIGN:	SQUADRON R/T AIRCRAFT CALL SIGN:
GROUP COLLECTIVE CALL SIGN:	
"TINSEL" FREQUENCIES:	CEASE JAMMING:
M.F. D/F SECTION(S) ALLOTTED:	
BASIC Q.F.E.	

FLIGHT PLAN		
POSITION	E.T.A.	FACILITIES AVAILABLE & ACTION

*   SQUADRON & NATURE OF FLIGHT TO BE ENTERED AFTER LANDING

---

letters in code. If you moved the code letters on the Syko board the de-coded letters would be revealed. Cadets had two hours of Morse before a break, when the NAAFI wagon would trundle along to provide them with tea and a scone known as a 'wad'. Some cadets found the Morse very difficult; all the dits and dahs could make a trainee suffer the 'doolally tap'. Those who could not master Morse were assigned to other duties. As well as listening to Morse code the cadets had to translate it visually using an Aldis Lamp. Cadet Mr. Geoff Floyd remembers spending the first few months of his training 'learning Morse code, learning to send and receive by Aldis Lamp, learning the rudiments of semaphore signalling, and learning basic knowledge of electrical and radio circuits, and how to operate wireless receivers and transmitters.' Cadets also received instruction in Radio Telephony, and the Station Commander sometimes monitored the training frequency, as one cadet who was caught pretending to be a racing car commentator found out to his cost! Examinations were ongoing to check the progress of cadets, the first — after three weeks — being a minimum of 12 words, the next exam required a minimum of 14 words per minute, then a few weeks later 16 words per minute. The final examination required 18 words per minute, although later courses demanded a minimum of 22 words per minute be attained. Cadets were permitted to sit each test three times. If the cadet failed every time he was dismissed from the course and given some other task on the base.

Technical tuition covered all areas of circuitry, electronics, valves, condensers, resistances and super-heterodyne radio. Mr. Bill Williams remembers his training included 'technical radio construction and operation and using the radio sets TR1082/ TR1083 then Marconi TR1154/R1155.' Cadets would have to

Date	Hour	Aircraft Type and No.	Pilot	Duty	REMARKS (including results of bombing, gunnery, exercises, etc.)	Day	Night
				Time carried forward :—			
26.11.43	08.30	DOMINIE X4456	08.30	Pupil W.op.	Rec. Tuning — TR 1082/1083	1.45	
"	10.30	"	10.30	"	Loop Manip	1.35	
2.12.43	08.40	X7500 W/op	W/O Lord	"	Loop Manip	1.40	
"	10.30	X7500	Sgt FitzGerald	"	Tuning by calib B Code	1.35	
11.12.43	13.35	PROCTOR HM475	Sgt. Palzer	"	No Ex.	.15	
20.12.43	08.55	DOMINIE X4439	F/S Lind	"	Tuning by calib Bbode	1.25	
"	10.40	"	"	"	Loop Manip	1.45	
22.12.43	13.25	X4439	F/S Lind	"	Back tuning	1.55	
"	15.30	"	"	"	NO EX. (prepared to bale out)	1.00	
8.2.44	16.10	PROCTOR HM432	Sgt Hall	"	Simple Com.	1.00	
10.2.44	9.05	HM322	F/S Lee	"	freq change.	1.00	
11.2.44	8.55	R4541	F/S Bratt	"	freq change	1.00	
"	13.50	DX198	F/S Lee	"	Simple Com.	1.10	
18.2.44	09.10	DX243	F/S Hope	"	" "	1.00	
"	15.20	LZ717	Sgt Duvall.	"	" " TR 1154/55.	1.00	

	Hrs.	Mins.
TOTAL FLYING HOURS:-	19	05

M.E. AIRCRAFT   S.E. AIRCRAFT
  12-40   6-25

CERTIFIED CORRECT

[signature] F/O

O.C. AIR OPERATING   TOTAL TIME ON   19.05

learn to strip the Marconi sets down to the basic components in fault finding exercises, then re-assemble them. Like Morse, cadets were regularly tested in all areas of technical knowledge. Tuition in RAF Procedure detailed the rules and regulations of networking, how to pass messages, and how to set up a radio network.

Aircraft recognition was a test of memory. Cadets had to know the wingspan and length of all enemy aircraft; if they went on to become a Wireless Operator / Air Gunner they would then be able to correctly aim at an enemy aircraft and hopefully ensure a direct hit by taking into consideration any side wind. Physical education was also a large part of their training. Sport activities in the afternoon were assigned, although it was not compulsory to attend the organised sports days, and some preferred to stay in the Nissen huts to write letters or poetry, a popular form of escapism amongst the cadets as it allowed them to express their feelings at the living conditions and boredom of life on base. Swimming played a large part of their physical instruction, as the RAF had lost many aircraft over water. Hereford pool was utilised for swimming training, and for instruction in how to inflate and paddle a dinghy, as most operational aircraft were fitted with these as a safety precaution. Other lessons included combat training, grenade practice using live grenades, rifle shooting, pistol shooting, firing sten and bren guns, bayonet practice, learning to operate a four gun turret fitted in a mock up aircraft, air to ground intercom systems, airfield lighting and approach systems and, as one cadet remembers, 'hygiene, and instruction of the problems in store for us if we consorted with loose women!'

Cadets would spend all day in lessons, and most of the evening studying their notes and technical books for the next day's instruction; but sometimes they were ordered on Guard Duty. This involved patrolling the perimeter of the base with a sten gun. Cadets on guard duty would patrol for two hours, then were given four hours off, and this pattern continued throughout the night. Cadets assigned to the duty still had to attend lectures the next day, and no reprieve was given if a cadet fell asleep in class. Mr. Bill Williams recalls that the three Wings took turns to do guard duty, but that the two smartest men on parade from the Wing whose turn it was were excused guard duty. Indeed Bill boasts that he only had to do it once.

In addition to the regular lessons, cadets were also required to participate in various drills and exercises. On 20 April 1942 and every month thereafter, the station had an anti-gas exercise. The duration of the exercise usually lasted until the following day. Gas masks had to be worn for hours at a time, which, as those who have ever worn one will know, would have been a horrible experience. The eye pieces of the gas mask would steam up, and despite personnel being issued with anti-mist paste to rub inside the eye pieces, it was never very effective. If the condensation was bothersome, the effort of puffing in and out was exhausting. Gas attacks were simulated by sirens sounding, and people waving hand rattles. Personnel would have to wait for the 'All Clear' before the masks could be removed.

Final board examinations were taken over two days; technical subjects and Morse code one day; semaphore with flags and radio telephony the other. Once a cadet had passed all the examinations he was awarded his sparks, the Wireless Operators badge, which depicted a hand grasping three flashes of lightening (see p.*iii*). The badge was to be sewn on the right sleeve of the uniform. Trained

Ground crew were paid an additional Trade Pay. If a cadet failed to get his sparks he would become a general duties airman.

During the early years of the Second World War, cadets that completed the Ground Wireless Operator course would be sent for six months or a year as a detachment to another RAF station in Bomber or Coastal Command, or be seconded to the Army. Then they would come back to RAF Madley to train as Air crew Operators. However, as the war progressed, Ground crew were needed in the air as soon as possible, so Ground crew were granted one week's leave before they embarked on the second stage of their training as Air crew cadets. This was altered again on 28 June 1943 with the start of a 'straight through' course in which cadets went straight into training as Air Signallers once ground training was completed. This combined course lasted 24 weeks, and RAF Madley was one of the first bases to adopt it.

When a Ground crew cadet who had already won his sparks was selected for Air crew cadet training he was given a white cap flash. An air crew cadet's introduction to aircraft was a mocked up radio compartment which was as realistic to the real thing as they could make it, even including engine noises inside. The cadets were then issued with flying kit, which caused a great deal of excitement, and a parachute – usually with the comment 'bring it back if it doesn't work and we'll exchange it!' Many cadets had never been inside an aircraft before. Groups of six cadets were loaded into a twin engine De Havilland Dominie known as a 'flying classroom' together with their instructor and the pilot, who was usually on a rest period from combat duties. Some cadets found the experience a less than pleasant one. Aircraft were equipped with a Smith's Crisps tin for airsickness which often proved inadequate. The phrase 'Carry the Can' (which originated in the 1920s) was often used on base, as the last cadet to use the Smith's tin had to carry the can to the latrine to empty it, whilst it was the job of the WAAF Flight Mechanics to clean inside the messy aircraft after a training flight. After a while they refused to do it, and the cadets responsible for the mess were made to clean the aircraft themselves. Many cadets suffered terribly with air sickness, and those who could not overcome it were eventually restricted to ground duties. Initial flights lasted for one hour to one hour 45 minutes, usually over the Malvern Hills, Hereford and Worcestershire. The instructor, pilot and cadets could communicate with each other and to base by means of earphones and a microphone built into their helmets. The instructor would explain to the cadets how to operate wireless sets in the air, and then each of the six trainees would take turns in sending and receiving messages to the WAAF ground crew at base, using the base call sign 7D7. However, more than once a poor trainee was left literally hanging in mid air desperately trying to contact the station, only to learn later that the WAAF ground crew had downed tools on hearing the station tannoy announce 'The time is now 12 hundred hours', which was the signal to go to lunch. Log books were kept of all messages transmitted or received, and these were closely scrutinised upon landing. The logs had to tally with the instructor's figures, so there was no chance of getting away with cooking the books.

After seven to ten days flying in Dominie aircraft, cadets advanced to the single engine Percival Proctors. The Mark I and Mark II Proctors had only room for the pilot and one trainee, so the cadet had the pressure of operating on his own. The Mark III and Mark IV, introduced at Madley later in the war, could take

A group of pilots at RAF Madley

two trainees. One of the cadet's first jobs once airborne was to unwind the aircraft's aerial, a 120 foot long wire cable which was not anchored within the aircraft, so if it was unwound too far it was lost to the four winds, and the cadet was charged ten shillings for the cost of a replacement. A trailing aerial could also be used to navigate by direction-finding. To do this the cadet would extend the cable behind the aircraft, tune the radio and transmit a Morse 'dah' on medium frequency to the ground crew. The signal would be homed in on by three different RAF stations. Using triangulation, the ground crew could then establish the aircraft's position and give the cadet a course to steer by. A good wireless operator would be able to direct the pilot anywhere; a good back up in a combat situation if the navigator was lost. The aerial could snag in the propellers, so cadets had to exercise extreme caution. Wireless Operator Mr. Reg Payne recalled that there was a large tree at the end of one of the runways the branches of which would become entangled with aerial wires which cadets had failed to wind in before landing. Periodically some poor cadet would have to climb the tree

Group Photos
Left: a group showing victory signs, (above) a photograph of a group of cadets that had qualified circa 1943/4 *taken in a Hereford photographers and (right) a mixed group of WAAFs and cadets of A & E Flights, August 1946*

The Proctor series of aircraft gained an excellent reputation during the War as the standard Fleet Air Arm and R.A.F. wireless training machines, also on communications work with all three Services.

Latest of the series, the Percival Proctor V is a low wing, four seater cabin monoplane of wooden construction. Leading edges of the wings, fuselage and tail plane are plywood covered, the remaining surfaces being fabric covered. Split flaps extend from ailerons to fuselage and each wing is hinged at the rear spar for folding.

A fixed undercarriage is used, comprising spring compression legs with oleo dampers, mechanical brakes and stream-lined spats over the wheels. The wide track is of great advantage on soft ground and when landing or taking off across wind. A fully rotatable shock-absorbing tail wheel unit is fitted.

With the de Havilland Gipsy Queen II engine, giving 208 h.p. for take-off, the Proctor V has an economical cruising speed of 140 m.p.h. Two 20-gallon petrol tanks are fitted, one in each outer wing, and suffice for a range of 500 miles. Two additional 10-gallon tanks can be supplied and are accommodated in the centre section. Oil is carried in a 5⅞-gallon tank in the starboard centre section, with an oil cooler to port.

Standard colour schemes are :

(1) Satin aluminium with red, blue or green flash and lettering ; leading edges, legs and spats to match or silver ;

(2) Fuselage turquoise, wings and tail silver, legs and spats turquoise or silver, dark blue lettering.

Interior : Grey leather and lining. Alternative colour schemes are available to order.

Luxurious accommodation for four persons is provided in the cabin, which is entered through large hinged doors at either side. The front seats are separately adjustable, whilst the rear seat extends full width, with a central folding arm rest and head rests. The cabin is soundproofed and is upholstered in leather and cloth, with carpeted floor.

Excellent all-round vision is provided by the large windscreen and windows. Ventilation is by controllable air inlets in addition to the sliding windows, whilst a cabin heater may be supplied as an extra. Sun blinds are fitted to all side and top windows. Luggage is carried behind the rear seats and there is also a locker at the rear for light articles.

All controls are most conveniently placed for operation by the pilot. The main instrument panel carries air speed indicator, altimeter, directional gyro, gyro horizon, turn and bank indicator, rate of climb descent meter, tachometer, manifold pressure gauge, oil pressure gauge, oil temperature gauge, fuel contents meters, vacuum gauge, voltmeter and clock. Electrical switches are carried on a fixed panel to port of the main panel. A magnetic compass is mounted on the cockpit floor and a fire extinguisher, connected by pipe line to the engine compartment but readily detachable for use in the cabin, is installed centrally.

Dual control is shown in the illustration and can be fitted at an additional cost of £25.

Standard equipment includes full night flying equipment, including landing lamps, navigation lamps, cockpit and instrument lighting. The airframe is completely bonded and the engine fully screened to permit the use of complete radio equipment, which, however, is not fitted as standard and entails some sacrifice in pay load.

PRINCIPAL DIMENSIONS

Span	..	39 ft. 6 in.	12 m.
Length	..	28 ft. 6 in.	8.6 m.
Height (tail up)	..	10 ft 8 in.	3.3 m.
Height (tail down)	..	7 ft. 3 in.	2.2 m.
Wing Area	..	202 sq. ft	18.77 sq. m.
Wheel Track ..	..	9 ft. 9 in.	3 m.
Tankage	..	40 gallons	182 litres

PRICE COMPLETE **£3,300** STERLING EX WORKS

Includes full blind and
night-flying equipment
(Radio extra)
Available for Immediate Delivery

and retrieve the tangled wire. Another Air crew cadet commented 'I think my left arm is now half an inch longer than my right one' which he claimed was due to winding and unwinding the heavy wire aerials! Pilots could be another concern to a young cadet. Mr. F. Day recalls one flight when the pilot knew his girlfriend was on the ground below. 'He started doing funny tricks for her to recognise him. I was scared stiff and we had to return to base

Above: A Percival Proctor in flight. Left a sales brochure for the aircraft just before the advent of the Second World War. From 1932 Percival aircraft set a variety of records: 1935 new record for flight from England to Australia (6 days, 21 hours, 19 minutes) in a Percival Gull; 1936 new record England to Australia (5 days, 21 hours — by Miss Jean Batten) in a Percival Gull, which she reduced by two and three-quarter hours the following year. 1936 also saw a race at Littorio Italy won by an Italian flying a Percival Vega Gull against 75 competitors representing 9 nations. In 1937 the record to Australia was reduced further, this time by H.F. Broadbent, in a Percival Vega Gull, to 5 days, 4 hours, 21 minutes.

because I could not get the radio to work. After we had landed an engineer came up to us, opened the door and switched the radio on. My face was red!' Another pilot always used to 'blip' the aircraft's engine as he flew over his girlfriend's house; she would run outside and wave a tablecloth in response.

Mr. Edgar Turner remembers an episode where a pilot nearly got him into trouble. 'On my first flight I received a coded set of letters repeated over and over again. When I looked in the instruction manual the code meant 'Return to base immediately' so I told the pilot. He asked me to query the base in plain language. I was told in no uncertain terms to 'Return to base immediately ... or else!' The pilot had taken the aircraft up before it had been cleared for flying by the ground crew. The pilot was told off for querying the order, but luckily Edgar was congratulated on picking up his first signal in the air.

If the weather permitted, cadets had two training flights a day, but in the winter more time was spent waiting on the ground than in the air. However, if the weather was fine, Mr. E.G. Jackson remembers that 'the Battle of Madley Circuit would occur almost hourly throughout the day. There would be twenty or thirty Proctors trying to land in a space of a few minutes, and each pilot tried to manoeuvre to the most advantageous position relative to other Proctors to make the final approach and landing without having to go around again.' He also recalls that some of the Proctors' propellers leaked oil which would form a fine film over the windscreen, and if visibility became too restricted pilots would complete the touch down by looking through an air vent that measured approximately 3 inches by 6 inches. An ambulance was always on stand-by when aircraft landed as accidents often

Some of the photographs that record the presence of WAAFs at RAF Madley, along with Pat Webster, a cook at the men's sickquarters, trying out her new bike in 1942/43 (top right)

occurred — over-running the runway or the occasional aircraft ending up in a hedge! One cadet recalled seeing two Proctors collide whilst manoeuvring in the circuit; he helped pull four dead crew members from the wreckage, something he has never forgotten. Despite these un-nerving moments, cadets needed as much time in the air as possible as they had to get used to operating the radio equipment in the confines of the aircraft. They also had to learn new skills such as locating the various radio beacons that constantly transmitted Morse code. Morse lessons still featured

Signal Section (WAAF) at RAF Madley.
From left to right: LACW (Leading Aircraft Woman) Tute,
LACW Lynch, LACW Ratnett, Cpl. Connop, ACW Whatley
and LACW Williams

heavily in the Air crew cadet course, as did examinations which were oral, visual, and written, and required a minimum pass mark of 40% for each subject. About a week after cadets successfully passed their final exams, they paraded in 'best blue' uniform and were presented with the 'S' brevet, wireless flash, and sergeant's stripes by the Station Group Captain. Air crew were then given a week's leave. On their return to RAF Madley they waited to receive details of their posting, usually initially to Gunnery School — often at Pembrey or Evanton.

Although the Ground crew and Air crew courses were demanding, life on base was not all studying and hard work. There were opportunities for the young cadets to enjoy themselves, and pay day was looked forward to with great anticipation. Pay parade occurred once a fortnight in one of the hangars. Cadets stood in rank before a wooden table that was manned by an officer, a pay clerk, and an NCO, who would bark out a name at which that man would spring to attention, march towards the table, salute the officer and recite the last few digits of his service number. With a few pounds to spend, the bright lights of Hereford attracted cadets, though it was a rare treat to have a night on the town. There was a bus service to Hereford that passed the base, although it was infrequent, and there were always long queues to get the last bus back from Hereford. If a cadet missed the bus it was a six and a half mile trek back to base, with the danger of being spotted by the Service Police who patrolled the country lanes at night trying to catch airmen still off base after the 10 o'clock curfew. Many a cadet avoided being put on a charge by diving into the nearest hedge on seeing the Service Police bicycle lights coming towards him, and it was just bad luck if there was a blackout in force. But it was worth the risk to enjoy a film at the Odeon cinema, such as *Gone with the Wind*, *Life and Death of Colonel Blimp*, *Gentleman Jim*, or *Phantom of the Opera*; made all the better if there was a girl to cuddle in the back row. A meal out was a special treat and the Servicemen's Canteen always provided a good lunch, or the Salvation Army Canteen, which was always popular as the volunteer staff would never refuse a cup of tea or a bun to a serviceman who hadn't got the penny that they each cost. There were also numerous cafés in the city, and a hungry serviceman could have a mixed grill if he could afford the 2s. 6d. price.

There was a dance nearly every night in Hereford, and on occasion the big bands were in town, such as Billy Cotton, Harry Gold, Billy Turner, and Joe Loss, who played at the Shire Hall. The Green Dragon also had dancing, as the ATS were billeted there, or, if a quiet drink was required, it offered comfortable surroundings, as did numerous other pubs in the city. One cadet remembered being told by officers that a particular pub was off-limits as it was an establishment of 'ill-repute'. He said at the time he thought the officers were looking after his well-being, but realised later that the pub was reserved for officers only and cadets were not welcome.

For those servicemen and women that did not want to travel into Hereford to socialise, Madley had two pubs within easy walk of the north-west side of the base. One cadet, Mr. W. Owen, remembers the Red Lion pub in Madley and 'the power of the local scrumpy cider — something new for a London boy.' But not all took to the local brew. Indeed, the strength of the cider took some by surprise, and one cadet remembers being too drunk one night to find his own billet, and spent some considerable time wandering around the base trying to find it. In his defence, personnel moved billets

frequently, and to find a particular Nissen hut to which you may have only recently moved, in the dark, and amongst the hundreds of other Nissen huts on site, would be a challenge even without the complication of alcohol! One cadet remembers that the effects of drinking locally brewed cider lingered for some time. It was not uncommon to see a cadet still slightly drunk the next morning, when a cup of tea, instead of reviving him, would bring back the effect of the alcohol. The local residents of the village frequented the Red Lion pub, so it was a good opportunity for servicemen and women to talk with the villagers. One local farmer used to drive a pony and cart to the pub and leave it outside while he enjoyed a few drinks. One day someone played a prank on him as, when he left the pub to return home, he found his pony had been turned the wrong way around in the shafts, and was facing the front of the cart!

Personnel billeted at site 1A were close to the Bull Ring pub at Kingstone and servicemen, when not on sentry duty, doing chores or homework, would sometimes have a drink there, or in the Mason's Arms at Gooses Foot. Cadets billeted on the far side of the base were not within such easy walking distance of the pubs, and many evenings were spent drinking cocoa made on the hut stove and swotting, or 'binding' as it was known, for the next day's lessons.

Entertainment could also be found on base for those who did not want to venture into Hereford. The camp cinema cost 3d. admission and dances occurred regularly in the camp dining hall and were often frequented by locals, and every Saturday night young ladies were bussed in from Hereford. At least one wedding was the result of these base dances. Mr. John Thorn served at

RAF Madley between 1942 and 1944 and in addition to training, he ran the cinema and ENSA shows. The base had a theatre, and personnel would sometimes put on live performances themselves, or sometimes professional touring shows and entertainers were booked. One cadet, Mr. E.G. Jackson, remembers seeing a play written by and starring Emlyn Williams.

Many personnel from the base enjoyed the beautiful countryside surrounding Madley, and walked or cycled around the area. To some cadets from the city, Herefordshire was still very old fashioned, and the rural way of life was slow. But Madley was relatively self sufficient with all the amenities a country village would need. There was a blacksmith, a shop and a newsagent, a butcher, a carpenter, a wheelwright, a motor engineer, a mason, the Red Lion, and other nearby pubs. Other services were provided by travelling craftsmen such as the cooper, who would arrive in the village to make the barrels needed for the cider making. Medical services were supplied by the District Nurse, who would cycle up to 40 miles a day to see her patients. Madley residents paid 1d. a month to get free attendance by the nurse, or 2d. per visit. The ladies of Madley helped the Red Cross provide medical supplies for the troops fighting on the front lines. The ladies would make bandages from sheets, rolling them, packing them and despatching to various Red Cross units. After the war, the Red Cross held a meal at the Red Lion to say thank you to all its helpers. Madley Women's Institute members also did their bit for the local war effort. They busied themselves knitting garments for the ATS, Army, and Air Force, darning socks and conducting lessons for the other ladies of the parish in Make do and Mend, and Wartime Cookery. The ladies of Madley also helped the servicemen with laundry and ironing, taking in uniforms and washing, starching and pressing them to the standard required. One local lady remembers taking in the uniforms of the French trainees stationed at RAF Madley. The French uniforms had stiff collars which were very difficult to iron, so to achieve the desired result she would put extra starch on the collar, fasten it around a pudding bowl, and bake it in the oven until it was dry.

RAF Madley was a multi-national station. Members of the Free French Air Force were billeted at No. 1 Wing. There was also a

RAF Madley ATC staff 1945
D. Willis LAC Bradley
Billet Officer (?) 2 Met Girls Fl Lt. Simmons SATCO

large contingence of Polish airmen who had fled their homeland as the Nazi invasion began. Australians, Canadians, New Zealanders, South Africans, Brazilians, and one Nigerian, Pilot Officer Flight Lieutenant E.P. Thomas (whose tragic tale will be told in a later chapter) were all based at RAF Madley. Foreign cadets would receive the occasional food parcel from their homeland and amaze the British lads by the exotic delicacies of their native country. In addition to the various allied nationalities, the base was also home to Italian, and, later, also to German, Prisoners of War. Mr. Geoff Meats, a local resident, recalls an escaped German pilot who hid in a barn 400 yards from RAF Madley perimeter fence. A farmer attending his cattle disturbed the pilot, who ran out. He was subsequently caught at Bridge Brook.

POWs were used as labourers in the fields, and farmers could hire POWs from the Ministry of Agriculture. The Ministry would deliver them to local farms by bus and return to collect them in the evening. The Ministry would even provide the POWs with a packed lunch so they would not need to stop working in the fields. Some farmers and their families who regularly used POWs as labour got to know them quite well. One family became quite friendly with a German prisoner of war who worked on their farm and used to let him come into the house to eat a hot lunch with them. Another German working at their farm asked if he too could join the family in the house, and refused to eat his lunch outside. The family, however, became suspicious of this prisoner, as it seemed as if he had an ulterior motive, and denied him access to their home. It was a common sight during the latter years of the war to see POWs being transported to and from farms by bus, often passing cadets who had to march everywhere on foot. No doubt some cadets were envious of the POWs' transport as they trudged on in the rain. Near Ross-on-Wye there was an unfortunate incident between POWs and three servicemen. It occurred at 5pm on the evening of 16 March 1943. Three servicemen were standing by the side of a road at Glewstone as a bus transporting German prisoners of war passed by. As the bus passed, one of the servicemen gave the prisoners the 'V' sign.

Three crew members together with a German Prisoner of War (top right), photographed in 1946

The bus then slowed to turn a corner, and several prisoners of war jumped off to confront the servicemen. The NCO in charge of the prisoners also jumped off the bus and demanded the servicemen's names for antagonising his prisoners, which they declined to give. The situation became heated, and the bus driver's plea for the prisoners to return to the bus went unheeded. In the argument that followed, the NCO reportedly hit one of the servicemen, which led to an all out brawl between servicemen, prisoners, and the NCO. The fight was only stopped when another POW got off the bus and managed to break up the fight and persuade the NCO and the prisoners to return to the bus. Not all encounters between servicemen and prisoners were so troublesome. After the Italians capitulated on 8 September 1943, the Italian POWs were allowed some responsibilities and duties on the base. By 1944 they were participating in fatigue duties, and in April 1945 a team of Italians training alongside the cadets came second in the anti-gas and fire drills, and enjoyed the odd game of football with the cadets. At the end of December 1946 there were still 60 POWs on site.

Some cadets would travel around the countryside and visit local farms to scrounge eggs, or exchange 12 bore cartridges for them, procured discreetly from rifle practise. Cadets would help out with odd jobs on the farm for a bit of pocket money, especially in September when hop picking required many labourers. It also provided cadets with a chance to meet some girls. Hops were often gathered by the Land Army girls, but young women who were employed in Hereford would travel to the farms to do a couple of hours hop picking in the evening. Farmers would help cadets by giving them a lift back to base on the back of a tractor, which was considered great fun, or letting cadets use their well in very hot weather as this was closer to some huts than the base's own supply. One farmer recalls a line of airmen with buckets and yokes carrying water from the well near his farm back to the camp. Mrs. P. Evans, a WAAF wireless operator, fondly remembers that one farming family, 'Mother' and 'Father' Crump and their sons and daughters always had an open house for servicemen and women; the Crumps' home offered a few comforts such as an open fire, and home cooked fare. One day, Mrs. Evans, whose duties were to receive Morse communications from the training aircraft, commented to her superior that she did not understand the conditions the cadets were faced with in the air. The next day, Mrs. Evans was amazed to find that her superior had arranged for her to go up in a Dominie to experience the receiving end of messages, after which other WAAF and ground staff were allowed an occasional flight in an aircraft. Cadets often tried to cadge joy flights from the pilots. Polish pilots stationed at RAF Madley would often oblige to relieve the boredom of a Sunday afternoon, and cadets would jostle to get aboard. Mrs. Lambert, who was a parachute packer and safety equipment worker, also recalls being taken for a joy flight by a pilot who was later to be her husband. He would take her up in a weather plane over the Black Mountains 'and do the loop-the-loop to try to make me sick'; but despite this she still married him!

Ground staff included the mechanics and carpenters who maintained the aircraft, which were partly made of wood and needed regular repairs. One veteran remembers that in very high winds the ground staff had to hang on to the wings of the aircraft to steady them and to stop them blowing away! Ground staff were

Certificates of Qualification.
(to be filled in as appropriate)

1. This is to certify that _Skinner M.D, 1709148_

    has qualified as _W. Op (aircrew)_

    with effect from _21 AUG 1943_ Sgd _____ F/Lt

    Date _21 AUG 1943_   Unit _No 4 R.S._

List of Certificates of Qualification,
this entry being for a cadet from Madley

also responsible for emptying the latrines into septic tanks on the back of a lorry, and other menial tasks. Cadets also had to help with some of the daily chores of the station. Every ten days or so they had to do a day in the Cookhouse, peeling potatoes, preparing food, and washing the very greasy pans without the aid of solvents or detergents. The Cookhouse would put out bread and cheese in the evening as a light supper, and cadets billeted in distant Nissen huts would take it in turns to cycle back to the Cookhouse to collect the rations for the whole hut. Mr. Bill Williams remembers spending Christmas Day 1943 on base, though he could not recall what delights the Cookhouse prepared for them. Christmas evening was spent at the station cinema, and, whilst he did not receive any leave over Christmas, he was given three days off duty. He was then given a 48-hour pass on 31 December to visit his family. He remembers 'on my way back to the station after the leave, the taxi I was travelling in had a flat tyre and I was 15 hours late getting back. I was put on a charge, but so many others were also late they dropped all the charges.' Bill and his fellow cadets were lucky that day. Cadets were frequently put on a charge for all sorts of reasons: lost socks, sheets, or other bits of kit, meant a certain charge, and maybe even a monetary fine to replace the missing article. Dirty boots or dull buttons on parade, and a host of other actions or inactions could land a cadet or WAAF on a charge that at the least would be a severe reprimand by their senior officer, or, at the worst, would mean extra duties, revoked privileges, or cancelled leave. One Warrant Officer was particularly disliked by the cadets, and they liked to play pranks on him. One day the cadets filled his wellington boots with water, but the Warrant Officer was unable to put anyone on a charge as nobody would own up to the stunt. To exact his revenge, the Warrant Officer made all the cadets go on parade in extremely muddy conditions leading to much falling over, trampling of hats into the mud and general comic behaviour.

The Operational Diaries

Events at the base were recorded in the Operational Diaries (now held at the National Archives in Kew, under the references AIR 28/511, AIR 29/724 and AIR 29/1851). They detail, on a daily basis, the activities and training exercises undertaken by the cadets, as well as providing a monthly summary of on-site entertainment, competitions and sporting events. The Diaries also record some of the more influential visitors to the base, the first of which was Anthony Eden, who arrived by aircraft in March 1942, before being driven to Hay-on-Wye. A few months later, Australian and Canadian officers came to inspect the troops. After the war, in January 1946, the Under Secretary of State, Mr. Ivor Thomas visited RAF Madley. However, the flight of Rudolf Hess is not documented, perhaps because such secret or sensitive information was recorded in appropriately restricted files. It is also interesting to note that there is no mention of VE Day or VJ Day, or indeed of any following celebrations. It must be borne in mind, therefore, that although the Diaries provide a good perspective into life on the base, they are restricted by the parameters of their remit to record daily activities, and are not a comprehensive account of all that transpired at the base. However, the Diaries are invaluable as they document the changes that occurred in the wider context of the progress of the war. Increases in aircraft and cadet numbers are linked to the increases in Luftwaffe attacks and bombings and heavy allied losses; decreases of personnel and the diversification of training are similarly linked to preparing servicemen and women to return to civilian life.

In the early days of the station's existence, the number of personnel on site was dictated by the physical resources available. As has already been noted, just two weeks after the first cadets arrived, the intake of trainees was suspended due to the lack of accommodation and essential facilities. The Diaries note that in February 1942 the weather improved allowing site construction to continue and the completion of domestic wings provided the necessary accommodation for the intake of cadets to be resumed. On 19 February, 74 new trainees arrived on the base. The same day, 59 cadets from the original intake in November 1941 finished the Ground Crew Wireless Operators course. This established the pattern for the coming year; new cadets would arrive the same day as others would leave the base. This constant arriving and departing was further complicated when, exactly one month after the resumption of intake of Ground Crew cadets, the first Air crew cadets arrived, numbering 299 personnel. From that point, the base saw weekly arrivals of Ground and Air crew and weekly passing out parades. The initial massive intake of Air crew is an indication of the tremendous pressure the RAF was under at the time. The suspension of cadet intake at the end of 1941 was a serious set back. On 7 December 1941 the Japanese attacked Pearl Harbour. The next day both USA and Great Britain declared war on Japan, stretching military resources further. There followed a series of blows against the Allied forces. On 15 February 1942, Singapore fell to the Japanese; 10 March saw Rangoon fall followed by the increasing threat of India being lost to the Axis forces; on 6 May, the Philippines surrendered; on 8 May, Germany began their

No. 2 ENTRY.

Cadets Douglas, S. Rees, C.E. Hill, J.F. Faulkner, D.H. Hunter, G.L. James, K.T. Scott, W. English, R. Barker, R.J. Aspinell, D.C.E. Bearryman, H.W. Atter, C.E.

Cadets Brunwin, A. MacAuley, J. Warburton, R. Purse, D.W.G. Daniels, A.J. Fretwell, D. Lowes, T.W. Nash, E.J. Peary, K.J. Elliott, F.W. Whitehead, A. Jenkins, R.F.

Cadets McLay, W.F. Lewis, D. Bailey, G. Skirrow, N. Cummings, F. Lappin, T.M. Cole, G. Woolt, M. Halstead, A. Barrass, D. Beck, M.F.G. Archibald, D.L.

Cadets Arthur, E.M. Bragg, D.A. Clothier, C.L. Holt, W.A.] Cadets Complin, C.H.W. Sykes, G.H. Smith, R. Pratt, K.

Sgt. A.J. Coles F/Sgt. A.J.G. Thomas S/Ldr. J.P.E. Pope (Commanding Officer) F/Lt. G.E.M. Bennett Sgt. A.E. Goddard

Cadets Hardy, G. Prosser, M. Morley, F. Lawson, T. Cadets Carr, J. Senior, A. Coultous, N. Heaven, D.H.

Photographs of the No.2 and No.17 Entries, giving an indication as to how numbers of cadets rose over time. The white flashes on the hats indicate that the cadets have passed the Air crew exams

Air Crew Cadets   No. 4 S.S., 1942

NO. 17 ENTRY.

Cadets D. F. Knight, D. J. Clarke, A. G. Nunn, B. Evans, J. H. Kirk, D. G. Prockter, K. Redman, A. R. Crookes, W. E. Cowell, R. E. Cook, R. A. Beak, G. R. Bartlett, G. V. Briggs, H. C. Bardsley, R. F. Cotgrove, F. W. Beck, J. J. Kirkwood, A. Lindley.

Cadets P. Grugan, R. F. Griffiths, M. R. Dore, J. Brown, S. K. Yates, P. G. Wiles, A. P. Smith, R. T. Eason, J. A. Lamb, F. G. Harris, R. S. Burr, A. L. Russell, I. Machell, R. H. Mankelow, W. Bingham, B E. Carmichael, J. H. Cooper.

Cadets D. Johnston, T. L. Malley, W. A. Owen, C. Morgan, A. E. Field, D. H. Morgan, A. Holmes, W. Raycraft, K. Kettle, G. H. Evans, C. W. Collins, R. Hanton, A. McCormack, H. Etherington, M. P. Keenan, N. A. Monk, F. R. Girling, J. Dixon.

Cadets N. T. Phelps, A. S. Ridpath, N. Roebuck, F. J. Sainsbury, C. Page, N. Thompson, F. Bottomley, R. Carr, L. Jacobson, S. H. Jenkins, J. McGlashan, J. Howlett. H. Johnston, P. C. Johnson, R. G. Owen, R. H. Gilmour, D. T. Rumfitt.

Cadets D. F. Thilman, R M. Millward, AC. T. W. Blake, AC. D. A. Jaycock]   [Cadets AC. J. C. Spencer, AC. E. W. Phillpott, L. Burke, R. Healey,
Cpl. J. Smith, Cpl. P. Wilson, W/O. G. J. Lord   P/O. F. D. Nicol   S/Ldr. A. R. Hungerford   F/Lt. L. S. Smith   Sgt. S. C. Adnitt, Sgt. W. Wheeler.
(Adjutant)   (Officer Commanding)   (O.C. "C" Squadron)

Cadets D. E. Steele, D. Weaver, J. E. Lovett, B. L. Leftley, H. Lomas, C. Pease, J. McLaren, W. Burns, G. Bowyer, A. C. Gillett, F. J. Young, R. White, A. Jordan, H. J. Phillips, G. Rees.

offensive in the Crimea; and by June, Rommel had taken Tobruk and had arrived at El Alamein. In response to the Axis attacks, the RAF launched massive air raids against German targets. On 30 May, one thousand British bombers dropped their explosive cargo on Cologne. Such large air raids demanded huge numbers of RAF personnel, and the need for qualified Airmen was urgent. Approximately 100 new recruits arrived every week for the Ground crew course, and similar numbers enlisted on the Air crew course. The staff and WAAF on the base had to cope with a constant stream of new young faces. Mrs. P. Evans, a WAAF at RAF Madley said 'all the Airmen I recall seemed to be named John, which led to some confusion, thus variations of the name were needed.' By July 1943 the two courses were amalgamated into one 'straight through' course to enable raw recruits to join active service after just 24 weeks of training. Over 20,000 cadets participated in courses during the five years RAF Madley was operational.

The Diaries record the flying hours achieved for each month. At first the hours are low; bad weather and limited personnel caused aircraft to remain grounded for long periods. But quickly the hours increased to an impressive figure; by February 1942, 233 flying hours are recorded, and by the following month the figure had almost doubled to 408 hours. As the intake of Air crew increased, so did the flying hours. The flying hours peaked in July 1944 with 7,902 hours in the air. The Proctor aircraft could only accommodate one cadet and the pilot. Each cadet had to achieve a minimum amount of flying time to pass the course, so the cadets were taken up individually to practise their Morse and direction finding techniques. The pilots would then land, the cadet would alight and his place was filled by the next waiting Air crew cadet.

During the summer, the airfield was in constant use for take offs and landings. A local resident, Mr. Allan Patrick, a boy during the war remembered the noise of aircraft from the base would start early every morning — 'you never needed an alarm clock!'

The Diaries also document training exercises and drills. In June 1942, the station was host to an Army exercise. The Army brought with them two Hurricanes, two Mustangs and three Tomahawks. A second Army exercise was conducted in October 1942, and a third in November the same year. In this exercise the Army mounted a practice 'attack' on RAF Madley. During the exercise, some Army personnel asked a local farmer to give them some food. Before the farmer knew what had happened, the soldiers had set up communication wires all over the farmhouse and established their field headquarters there. The soldiers even spent the night at the farm. The next morning, some of the soldiers were shaving in the farm pond when they spotted a real enemy aircraft overhead. The farmer had to put up with their presence until the all clear was given later in the afternoon.

RAF Madley personnel also co-operated with the Home Guard in mock 'attack' exercises. The Home Guard would use potatoes as replica hand grenades, and stones shaken in a tin can represented machine gun fire. In one exercise, Madley Home Guard personnel managed to 'capture' RAF Madley HQ by launching a 'potato grenade' attack; a proud moment for the local lads! Madley Home Guard comprised a unit of approximately 30 men which conducted target practice in Moccas Park; an old oak tree there is still full of lead from their bullets.

RAF Madley personnel also conducted exercises with the local fire brigade. In December 1942 a joint exercise was undertaken to establish whether there would be enough water on the base to extinguish a major fire, for there had already been a couple of minor fires on the base. The first of these occurred on 18 April 1942, when a fire broke out on the north side of the aerodrome. Bales of straw had been used to camouflage tins of paint. The bales caught fire and the entire paint store went up in flames. A second fire occurred in a vehicle just a few days later. There was concern that if the base came under attack and the stores of aviation fuel

Madley Home Guard (Signals Section, 4th Battalion Herefordshire Regiment Home Guard)
Back row: Pte. J. Ruck, L/Cpl. W. Davies, Pte. D.G. Morgan
Middle row: Ptes. W.R. Skyrme, H.T. Portman, L/Cpl A. Davies, Ptes. P.B. Millichamp, S.S. Jones, T.J. Guy, E.W. Hughes
Front row: L/Cpl. F.E. Watts, Cpl. J.A. Edwards. Lt. D. Parsons (Signalling Officer) Cpl. W.H. Jenkins, Pte. R.G. Brookes

were ignited, there could be a major disaster. The exercise with the fire brigade concluded that a major fire could indeed be dealt with effectively but, thankfully, this conclusion was never put to the test. The aviation fuel did, however, have an unexpected secondary use, as Bridget Pring-Mill, a WAAF aircraft mechanic recalled. 'A duck landed in a quantity of waste oil. We used aviation fuel to clean it up, and released it back onto Madley pond. It sank.' The fuel had stripped its feathers of all natural oils, which affected its buoyancy. They kept the duck in the Sergeants Mess for three weeks before trying it again. That time it floated.

The Diaries document training other than in wireless and Morse, the type providing an indication of the wider events of the war. In May 1942, a two-week Field-craft and Weaponry course was conducted, to provide crew with some basic survival skills should their aircraft be shot down over enemy territory. In March 1943, personnel attended a course on tropical medicine, a response to the conflicts in Burma, the Pacific and New Guinea. Further courses in tropical medicine were conducted in 1944 and 1945. By late 1943, the station staged a monthly 'Chemical Warfare Day' in anticipation of potential attack. In May 1944, all leave was cancelled in preparation for Operation Overlord and the D-Day landings. In November the same year, personnel were trained in escape techniques. The RAF had learned that escapees from enemy incarceration could impart valuable information on the strength and location of Axis positions. Exercises in battle noise were also introduced at this time to prepare trainees for what was to come. By February 1945, training also included 'Mines and Boobies' tuition in reaction to the changing nature of warfare. The cadets were given demonstrations in street fighting and judo, and from April 1945, jungle warfare techniques were taught until the end of the war, obviously with the continuing battle against the Japanese in mind.

The development of radar also had an impact on the station. Mr. Geoff Meats, a local villager, remembers as a boy walking to school and finding many pieces of tin foil lying about. From February 1945, RAF Madley conducted radar tests, part of which involved the dropping of foil from aircraft, the foil creating a 'cloud' from which it proved difficult to pick out actual aircraft. Foil was also used as an SOS if communications had gone down on an aircraft, with drops being made every two minutes. Some school children would collect the foil and return it to the base. By April, a basic radar laboratory had been set up to train cadets in radar operation.

The role of the WAAF also changed during the war. Initially, there was only one member of the WAAF on site. By the end of March 1942, the WAAF personnel numbered 27; a month later, 86. Their numbers peaked in November 1944, when 478 WAAF are recorded at RAF Madley. It is also noted in the diaries that the same year, 400 new WAAF shoes made from recycled boots were delivered. Initially, the role of the WAAF was mainly administrative; however, as the demand for male personnel to enter battle increased, the WAAF stepped in to fill some of the traditionally male occupations. In March 1943, WAAF personnel took over the duties of Wireless Operators on the ground, and their performance was noted in the Operational Diaries as 'generally capable and conscientious'. At the same time, the cadets' training was reduced by a significant six weeks in another attempt to get cadets qualified and into active service as soon as possible. Other positions held by WAAF personnel included Flight Controller, Morse Tutor, Administration, Telephonist, Cook, Nursing staff, and Aircraft Mechanic. The duties of the WAAF Aircraft Mechanics included doing test flights after they had completed any maintenance on an aircraft. One WAAF remembered that she was feeling unwell after she finished working on an aircraft, to the extent that her friend, also an Aircraft Mechanic, offered to take her place on the test flight. Tragically, the aircraft crashed, her friend was killed, and the WAAF who was ill felt tremendous guilt.

Mrs. Phyllis Pitt was a WAAF Medical Orderly stationed at Madley between 1941 and 1944, whose duties included attending the victims of aircraft crashes. She would also administer inoculations to lads who were preparing for duties overseas. She recalls 'it was surprising how many passed out at the sight of a needle or blood!' Mrs. Pitt also remembers Hartley's Jam Factory next to the aerodrome. The workers would ask her how many patients she had. The workers would then send over fresh strawberries for all those in Sick Quarters. WAAF personnel were billeted near Kingstone Church, and the road between the billets and the bus stop became known as 'WAAF Lane'. Mrs. Bet Macklin was delighted to be posted to RAF Madley, as she was originally from nearby Clehonger. She was able to live at her mother's house on the edge of the station, and in the mornings she only had to pop over the aerodrome fence to report for work. Sadly, Mrs. Macklin lost two brothers in the war; their names are on the commemorative plaque in Madley church. Diana Elvidge was a WAAF telephonist at Madley. She recalls 'cycling around the countryside on days off and collecting milk each morning from the farm for their tea'. Others in their spare time would go scrumping for apples in the local orchards to supplement their food rations.

During their free time, personnel could enjoy organised sport and entertainment, and the Diaries detail these activities. Sport was actively encouraged to increase cadets' fitness, and active pastimes also went some way towards combating energies spent pursuing less wholesome physical activities! From November 1942, cadets were offered a range of sporting events, including boxing matches and soccer games. By the following January, rugby, hockey and cross country were also being organised, and the Fagan Cup was introduced, an inter-Wing competition for the combination of boxing, cross-country, soccer and rugger. This contest proved very popular, and the following month the station hosted 15 games of soccer. Badminton was introduced as the weather improved, and by the spring, cricket matches, tennis tournaments, cycling races and a cross-country championship were held. In June, cricket proved so popular that a new ground was opened. In August 1943, RAF Madley won the coveted Inter-Station Athletics competition. The station obviously had a selection of good footballers, as in November 1944 an RAF Madley team won the Hereford County Cup. WAAF personnel also enjoyed sport, and they formed a netball team in February 1944, and in June 1945 established a women's soccer team. In the winter months, when the weather was not suitable for many outdoor activities, table tennis and darts leagues were set up.

In May 1944, the US Army was given facilities at RAF Madley for Morse code practice, the American personnel encouraging other sports such as softball. A month later, the American General Patton arrived at RAF Madley. He was given a guard of honour and entertained with boxing matches between American and British personnel. The international bouts proved popular and the

No 3 Wing: Fagan Trophy Winners , March 1943
Back row: A/Cs J.D. Foulkes, D.M. Hogg, F.W.J. Webb,
R.T. Roxburgh, R.C.G. Hughes, LAC J. Leonard, G.W. Brown
Third row: A/Cs J. Stevenson, D. Hitchen, Cpl. C.W. Smith,
A/C J.C. Macara, Cpl. R.C. Doughty, A/Cs S. Bullock, A. Corsfoot
Second row: A/Cs J.D. Francis, J. Couch, R.J. Forbes,
A. Anderson, A. Wright, Sgt. F. Price, A/C C.T.F. Willard
Front row: Sgt. J.W. Murray (Trainer), F/Lt. G.E. Meredith (Physical Fitness
Officer), S/Ldr. A.R. Hungerford (Officer Commanding), P/O F.W.T. Fuller
(Adjutant), Sgt. G. Cowan (Trainer)
In front: A/C S.H. Bates

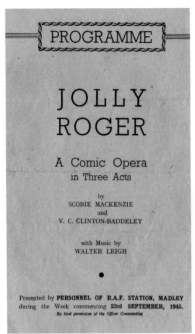

PROGRAMME

JOLLY
ROGER

A Comic Opera
in Three Acts

by
SCOBIE MACKENZIE
and
V. C. CLINTON-BADDELEY

with Music by
WALTER LEIGH

●

Presented by **PERSONNEL OF R.A.F. STATION, MADLEY**
during the Week commencing 23rd **SEPTEMBER, 1945.**
By kind permission of the Officer Commanding

Concert programme cover

competition was repeated in February 1945. Swimming was also well attended. Cadets were given swimming instruction at Hereford pool, and some personnel enjoyed the activity so much they competed in swimming galas in Abergavenny and Hereford, where they were champions of the meet. RAF Madley also won the Golf Cup in 1945; the inter-station revolver and grenade competition; and the rifle competition, adding to the station's record of sporting achievements. The base also held an annual Sports Day, which was attended, in 1944, by Air Vice Marshal J.R. Cassidy CBE and Mrs Cassidy, staff officers from headquarters, the mayor of Hereford and local villagers.

Local residents and people from Hereford city would also attend the dances and other entertainment at the station. By November 1942, the base had established a very full programme of entertainment. In that month alone 20 lunch concerts, 6 variety shows, 3 band concerts and 3 ENSA shows were performed. In addition, 18 dances were held and 12 films were screened. By April 1943, the station had secured a loan of £5,000 from the Air Ministry to open a cinema on site. The number and type of entertainment varied month by month, but a high level of entertainment was sustained throughout the war. In February 1944, the station held a total of 32 dances, and frequently over 60 films were shown during one month. Some films were even screened in French to accommodate the French speaking personnel. Other activities were also offered: whist drives, plays, gramophone recitals, musicals, ballet performances and revues were all provided for the entertainment of personnel and local visitors. The station had a brass band, and in 1942 the Diaries record the purchase of new instruments. Personnel organised their own amateur dramatics club, and members not only staged productions such as *Rope*, but used the facilities for piano lessons and costume design. Some personnel participated in the famous Three Choirs Festival in Hereford and others enrolled in bell ringing classes held at Kingstone. The base even formed a male voice choir, and a regimental concert party. Art and photography were encouraged, and a photographic exhibition was displayed in 1944, in the Information Room. The Diaries record, however, that by 1946, photography courses were cancelled due to lack of interest. Art lovers were no doubt thrilled when, in 1943, the National Gallery temporarily re-housed some of its fine art collection in Hut 66. Major galleries and museums adopted a policy of hiding precious artworks outside London for fear of Luftwaffe bombing raids.

Gardening was another popular pastime and personnel were encouraged to grow their own produce. Regular gardening competitions were held. In October 1943, the station won second prize in the local Horticultural Show for growing marrows, and also a 'Highly Commended' certificate for the garden in general.

In July 1944, RAF Madley won the Gardening Cup. The station usually had a large range of activities on offer, but in January 1945, all entertainment and sport was cancelled due to five days of heavy snow. 150 men were employed in snow clearance, and the only entertainment provided after a freezing day's work was to read one of the 2,500 books available from the library.

As the war progressed, preparations for demobbing servicemen and servicewomen began. The local population also contributed to the preparations. In May 1945, residents of Madley village raised an impressive £50 for the Welcome Home Fund, which had been established to give each returning serviceman or woman a wallet containing £5, as a thank you for their efforts. RAF Madley personnel also contributed by organising a fundraising darts match. Money was raised for the RAF Benevolent Fund too, by holding a sponsored gymkhana and horticultural show in September 1945. In 1946, a football match between officers and NCOs raised a massive £400 for charity; the losers had to contribute further to the charity, but to soften the blow an evening of 'housey housey' and an all-ranks dance was organised.

Preparations for the end of the war were not limited to such jovial activities, as everyone was encouraged to learn new skills in preparation for life after the war. In May 1944, WAAF personnel attended domestic science and shorthand classes in Hereford. In August 1944, WAAF and RAF personnel attended free evening classes in the city. The following month, the County Council offered courses in art, woodwork, typing and leatherwork. In October, personnel were encouraged to start correspondence courses and a self-tuition room was provided. In November, an entry in the Diaries proves that the room was not successful; it

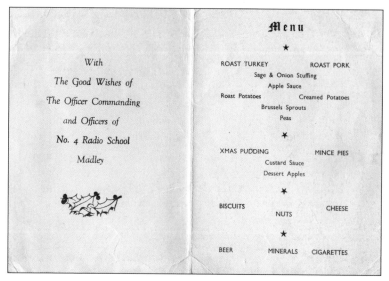

Christmas Dinner, 1944

notes 'no-one is attending'! As the war drew to a close, personnel were encouraged to think about future occupations. Courses were offered in advanced cookery to provide the skills needed in the hospitality industry. By April 1945, many officers and airmen were enrolled in courses that would prepare them for civilian life. In May 1945, just after VE Day, lectures were given on post war resettlement. By June 1945, over 300 personnel were undertaking a correspondence course. Lectures in Local Government were given, and were compulsory to attend. By November 1945, 265 staff at the base had been interviewed and advised on post war occupations. After the conflict had ceased, City and Guilds courses were offered in trades such as welding, electrical skills and communications.

Service and Release Book for Air Cadet R.W. Tilyard when he left Madley

November 1945 saw the upper age limit for air crew reduced to 30 years; anyone aged 45 and below could apply for redundancy. By January 1946, the Air Ministry ordered half the personnel be made redundant. The following month, all French personnel stationed at Madley were repatriated, and a month later, half of all cadets were redundant. April 1946 saw the beginning of the clean-up operation. The site was cleared of all unnecessary bedding: 4,500 blankets, 2,650 bolsters, and 1,800 mattresses were taken away, and 2,000 blankets were laundered. The site was cleaned and 200 lorry loads of refuse were removed and between 800 and 1,000 rats were killed. By May 1946, all Air cadets and Air Wireless Operators who had not applied to extend their service, were made redundant. Herefordshire County Council was desperate to recruit school teachers, and offered a fast track placement to any personnel interested. In July, the laboratories were stripped and removed, and by September other buildings were dismantled and transported to RAF Swanton Morley, the station that was to absorb the remnants of RAF Madley. Mr. Bill Williams and Mr. Malcolm Staves retrieved one of the bricks from No. 2 Wing as a memento; Bill still has one half of the brick, and Malcolm the other. On 23 September 1946, some of remaining personnel transferred to Swanton Morley. All personnel were engaged in the dismantling and packing of buildings and equipment, until RAF Madley was no more.

Tragedy Strikes

The gently rolling hills around Madley border the dangerously steep-sided Black Mountains and Brecon Beacons, and within minutes of being airborne, a pilot could find himself flying over this rugged and potentially deadly terrain. Climatic conditions in the Welsh mountains are notoriously changeable; a single day can see weather of all seasons, and snow and fog can descend without warning. Today, the SAS train in these mountains, the harsh environment testing the physical and mental strength of these elite troops. As RAF Madley pilots were conducting numerous flights per day, often over the Welsh mountains, it could be said that tragic accidents were almost inevitable. In the early years of the war, the response to an aircraft crash in the mountains was limited; personnel were ill equipped, and training was not specialised for mountainous conditions. But experience was soon gained, at a high cost, and rescue teams became expert in dealing quickly and efficiently with casualties in remote and isolated places. By 1944 RAF Madley had a permanent Mountain Rescue Unit of highly equipped and trained men. The Unit shared their knowledge of dealing with aircraft crash victims with other services such as the police and Home Guard, and from March 1945 training sessions occurred each month. The Unit was not only responsible for crashes involving Madley based aircraft, but also any other aircraft that came down in Radnorshire, Breconshire, Monmouthshire, or Herefordshire.

The following details of crashes and accidents have been sourced from the Operational Diaries held at the National Archives, Kew. These tragic incidents either involve aircraft from RAF Madley, or RAF Madley personnel responding to crashes of aircraft from other bases. Some incidents were minor, others resulted in fatalities. Additional information and eye witness accounts have been included where possible.

07.01.42   Two minor crashes, one in a Dominie, one in a Proctor as pilots were having difficulties with the wind on landing.

19.03.42   Proctor damaged on landing in bad weather.

20.03.42   Proctor damaged on landing in bad weather at Castle Farm, Madley due to engine failure.

21.03.42   Proctor did a forced landing near Abergavenny.

03.04.42   Dominie damaged after landing.

04.04.42   Proctor damaged after landing.

14.04.42   Dominie damaged after landing. Proctor damaged while taxiing.

16.04.42   Wellington from another base made a forced landing and was repaired at Madley.

25.04.42   Proctor damaged on landing.

28.04.42   Proctor damaged on landing.

29.04.42   Wellington made a forced landing near Madley when its starboard engine failed.

08.05.42   Tomahawk damaged on landing.

20.05.42   Ambulance sent to Radnor to collect casualties of a crashed Wellington, patients taken to Hereford hospital.

28.05.42   Proctor made a forced landing at Withington, Hereford

02.06.42   Two Proctors collided on the runway.

07.06.42   Halifax crashed in flames at Courtfield Farm, Lower Lydbrook near Ross-on-Wye. 11 fatalities. An Inquest into the crash took place on 23.06.42.

30.06.42	Proctor damaged in landing.
07.07.42	Wellington crashed at Llangrove after clipping a tree top near Ross-on-Wye, all crew were taken by ambulance from Madley to hospital.
27.07.42	Dominie slightly damaged.
18.08.42	Proctor hit another whilst taxiing, no casualties.
22.08.42	Master aircraft did a forced landing at Builth Wells, no casualties.
22.08.42	Halifax crashed at Builth Wells, no casualties.
03.09.42	Proctor did a forced landing due to engine seizure, no casualties.
06.09.42	Two proctors collided in mid air. All occupants killed, two pilots and two cadets. Chris Davis remembered the two Proctors collided just 25 metres from the school. Mr. Bettington recalls that one of the Proctors lost its tail and spun over and over. One fell by the woods and burst into flames.
13.09.42	Proctor collided with another while taxiing, no casualties.
03.10.42	Proctor burst a tyre during take off, no casualties.
12.10.42	Master aircraft crashed near Clyro, 1 fatality.
15.10.42	Proctor made a forced landing at Crowle, Worcester due to bad visibility and low fuel.
19.10.42	Proctor propeller hit the right forearm of an airman who was taken to RAF Credenhill hospital.
23.10.42	Proctor tipped on its nose on landing, no casualties.
03.11.42	Proctor made a forced landing 2 miles north of Madley due to engine trouble, no casualties.
03.11.42	Proctor made precautionary landing near Worcester due to bad visibility, pilot and cadet injured.
13.11.42	Proctor made a forced landing at Coleford, extensive damage but no casualties.
04.12.42	Mustang crashed at Ledbury, one fatality.
08.12.42	Dominie tipped on nose on landing, propellers damaged.
21.12.42	Proctor forced off runway by a cross-wind and tipped on nose, no casualties.
21.01.43	Proctor made a forced landing near Ledbury. Pilot okay, cadet injured.
21.01.43	Proctor overshot aerodrome at Broxbourne, Essex. Aircraft damaged, no casualties. (Aircraft occasionally flew from Madley to other bases, sometimes so that cadets could receive specialist training.)
03.02.43	Proctor tipped on nose while landing, no casualties.
04.02.43	Proctor tipped on nose while taxiing, no casualties.
20.02.43	Proctor on landing swung out and the undercarriage collapsed, no casualties.
25.02.43	Proctor while taxiing struck an ambulance, no casualties.
05.03.43	Proctor broke undercarriage on landing, no casualties.
06.03.43	Proctor hit another when taxiing, no casualties.
07.03.43	Proctor caught fire, no casualties.
12.03.43	Proctor hit Dominie when taxiing, no casualties.
15.03.43	Dominie did a successful forced landing at Bluntingthorpe[?] after engine failure, no casualties.
24.03.43	Proctor tipped on nose, no casualties.
28.03.43	Proctor collided with another on landing, cadet injured.
08.04.43	Proctor hit another while taxiing, no casualties.
12.04.43	Mid air collision between a Dominie and a Proctor, two pilots, one NCO and six cadets killed.
17.04.43	Dominie engine cut out at 5,000 feet, no casualties.
17.04.43	Proctor hit a tree on low descent, no casualties.
18.04.43	Proctor had very bad engine vibrations which caused a forced landing at Worcester, no casualties.
20.04.43	Proctor hit HM350[?] while taxiing, no casualties.

Dominie aircraft on the runway at Madley

22.05.43   Proctor hit another while taxiing, no casualties.

06.06.43   Dominie made a forced landing due to engine failure, no casualties.

12.06.43   Proctor hit another while taxiing, no casualties.

13.06.43   Dominie did forced landing due to engine trouble, no casualties.

26.06.43   Proctor knocked down an airman as he ran across the perimeter track while the plane was taxiing. The Proctor was left where it was on the perimeter and was then hit by another Proctor as it tried to pass. No casualties for either incident.

27.06.43   Proctor and Dominie collided in mid air, minor damage, no casualties.

08.07.43   Proctor made a forced landing at Little Peterstow farm due to engine failure when the pilot forgot to switch to port tank when the starboard tank ran dry, no casualties.

13.07.43   Proctor tipped on nose while taxiing in high winds, no casualties.

16.07.43   Oxford crashed on take off, pilot and two passengers injured.

31.08.43   Dominie tipped on nose at Worcester, no casualties reported.

31.08.43   Proctor tipped on nose, pilot injured.

01.09.43   Dominie overshot runway at Worcester and crashed on adjoining road, no casualties.

07.09.43   Proctor hit offices while taxiing, two ground crew injured.

11.09.43   Proctor aircraft went into an uncontrollable spin and crashed near two women picking potatoes at Rhos Fawr Common near Brecon, pilot and cadet killed.

16.09.43   US Army Air Force Flying Fortress crashed near Abergavenny killing all 10 on board, RAF Madley personnel took the bodies to Newport. Gordon Pembridge, then a 10-year-old boy at a farm near where the Flying

Fortress crashed, remembered airmen coming from Madley to guard the wreckage and recover the crew. They were billeted at the farm. Aircraft Number 425903 named 'Ascend Charlie'.

21.09.43 Proctor burst tyre on landing and tipped on nose, no casualties.

21.09.43 Cadet hit by wing of Proctor.

04.10.43 Dominie wing hit a cyclist.

11.12.43 Proctor knocked down two personnel while taxiing.

13.12.43 Proctor made a forced landing due to haze, no casualties.

13.12.43 Proctors collided on the perimeter track, no casualties reported.

13.12.43 Proctor knocked down two French cadets while taxiing, no casualties reported.

24.12.43 Two Proctors collided in mid air, one made it back to Madley but the other plunged down the mountainside of Mynydd Llangorse and ended up at a farm. Canadian pilot and his French cadet were both killed.

24.12.43 Proctor hit telephone wires when low flying, no casualties.

14.01.44 Wellington from Upper Heyford made a forced landing on the base at 01.30 hours. The crew of four baled out, but the pilot landed the aircraft safely although the plane overshot the runway. Crew flew out on 30.01.44.

30.01.44 Proctor crash, reason unknown, the pilot and cadet killed.

16.02.44 Two Proctors collided in mid air, one pilot and passenger killed, other pilot and passengers baled out. One airman

Two pictures of groups of cadets and WAAFs (above including newly qualified Air crew cadets) with fire tenders as a backdrop

noted in his diary 'Joe Peterson gone for a burton, Wade baled out.'

17.04.44   Dominie guided home by ground W/T operator due to bad visibility.

04.05.44   Proctor[?] aircraft crashed near Coleford, plane exploded, pilot and cadet killed. A day after this crash, a structural fault was discovered on the Proctor Mark IVs and all were immediately temporarily grounded.

24.08.44   US Liberator crashed.

20.11.44   Wellington crashed.

25.12.44   A Liberator named Bold Venture 111 crashed at Lower House Farm on Vowchurch Common near Madley. A fruitless search was made for her missing crew. It was discovered later that they had all baled out over Belgium assuming that their flak-damaged aircraft was about to crash. It flew back on its own.

12.01.45   Proctor crashed at Corn Du on west side of Brecon Beacons due to strong winds and adverse weather conditions while descending through thick low cloud. The pilot did not ascertain his position or request a controlled descent pattern. It is thought that the pilot dropped down below the cloud to pin point his position and then could not regain altitude. The port wing struck the mountainside. The pilot was Flight Lieutenant E.P. Thomas. He was the son of a Nigerian prince and was reputedly the only Nigerian flying with the RAF at the time. He was known by the nick name '23:59' and was a popular character on the base, as he would entertain his fellow airmen by doing tribal African dances after having a few drinks. He had had a few accidents prior to this, and some joked that his father paid for all the aircraft he damaged. He died at the scene.

The young cadet on board was W/T Op Trainee AC2 Frank Stokes. He suffered concussion and several injuries. On coming to, Frank tried to make the unconscious pilot as comfortable as possible then set off over the desolate snow covered mountain to find help. Frank survived by walking for miles through the snow and negotiating several streams to finally reach the Storey Arms Youth Hostel on the Brecon to Merthyr road. Frank was taken to hospital, but unfortunately by the time a rescue team reached Flight Lieutenant Thomas, he was dead.

06.02.45   Proctor crashed due to bad visibility. Pilot tried to make a forced landing, pilot and French cadet killed.

24.02.45   Aircraft crash east of aerodrome, two slight injuries.

29.05.45   Proctor crashed on Egdon Hill near Bromyard, three sustained head and jaw injuries.

07.06.45   Proctor made a forced landing, no casualties.

06.09.45   Proctor crashed after spinning out of control on a farm between Callow and Aconbury, three killed.

08.01.46   Mountain Rescue called out due to an Oxford that crashed on Hay Bluff near Capel-y-ffyn. Two crew rescued, one killed.

30.09.46   Hornet crashed on Brecon Beacons at a farm at Penderyn, pilot killed.

24.10.46   Proctor on night flying exercise collided with the tail of another when taxiing out, no casualties.

12.11.46   Mustang was carrying out a slow roll manoeuvre but the roll was too slow and the aircraft stalled and dropped the starboard wing which clipped the ground and broke the undercarriage, no casualties.

Several Wellington aircraft crashed in the area. One local resident, Mr. G. Meats recalls one Wellington that had been on a bombing mission to Germany. The Wellington came over RAF Madley aerodrome and made a belly-flop ditching near the perimeter in a cornfield. One chap had a broken leg and Mr. Meats' father rescued him. They buried the bombs and ammunition on site. Mr. Meats and a friend later found one bomb just under the surface and took it home, where it was promptly confiscated and dealt with. This field was later ploughed, and had this bomb not been found, it might have been hit by a blade of plough and exploded, as it was so near the surface.

Another local resident, Mr. D. Lewis recalls that a German plane, a Dornier, flew over the area, fired its machine guns, then bombed a factory. The German navigator used the River Wye, which shone silver at night, to find their target. Mr. Lewis says he also saw Messerschmitts and Stukas in the area. Other local reports of crashes, which, it must be recorded, are generally hearsay and can not be relied on as completely factual, include a Dominie that made a forced landing by a pub in Hereford, and another that crashed when its wing hit the ground; a Proctor that crashed in Hereford killing the pilot and cadet; a crash in the Brecon Beacons that was guarded by RAF Madley personnel; a Wellington bomber with Polish crew crashed at RAF Madley; and one Proctor that crashed in Harold Street, Hereford, and another that crashed near Eign Road on what was then the Air Training Corps Headquarters. The aircraft is reputed to have struck a tree and landed in an orchard, the aircraft catching fire and three people being killed. A witness remembers seeing chickens running around with their feathers on fire.

A more certain story is of Lancelot Steele Dixon who, on the day he gained his RAF wings, flew over his mother and step-father's house at Winforton. As he did so, he lost control of the plane, crashing in a nearby field and being killed outright.

Once the cadets of RAF Madley won their sparks and graduated to active service, there were many more losses to their ranks. Mr. Bill Williams knew seven fellow cadets who were killed, either in collisions, accidents or in operations.

Rudolf Hess and Madley

The story of Hess is still shrouded in controversy; there are numerous rumours, conspiracy theories, and suggestions of madness, foul play, and even murder. Below is a summary of the most probable story of Rudolf Hess and his stay in Britain.

Hess was born in Alexandria in Egypt on 26 April 1894 to a reasonably wealthy family as his father was a businessman. Hess moved to Germany and joined the military, subsequently fighting in the First World War and was twice injured, once from a rifle bullet that passed straight through his body causing two ribs to break and a lung to collapse. This injury left Hess with scarring on the entry and exit sites of the bullet, scars which become important facts later in the story.

After the First World War, Hess became a pilot, and later studied at the University of Munich. He joined a secret anti-Semitic political organization that believed in the supremacy of the Nordic races, and subsequently joined the Nazi party on 1 July 1920 after hearing Hitler give a speech in a beer hall. Hess was only the sixteenth member of the fledgling party, and was to become one of Hitler's most devoted followers. Hitler and Hess were both arrested after a failed attempt to seize power in Germany.

Hitler believed that the German Government was unworthy of power as it had left the country weakened after the First World War, and gradually recruited 'storm troopers' loyal to him and his Nazi ideology. On 8 November 1923, some 3,000 people gathered in a beer hall to hear three top government officials speak: the Bavarian Commissioner, the head of the Bavarian police and the head of the Bavarian army. Hitler chose the moment to surround the hall with his storm troopers before bursting through the door, shooting into the air. The crowd were kept in the hall, whilst the three officials were ushered into an adjoining room and given a choice: they could support his claim as the new leader and his plan to march on Berlin, or be shot. They agreed to join with Hitler. Hitler, Hess and Göring then set about taking control of Munich, but met with resistance from state soldiers and after a brief gun fight, Hitler and Hess were arrested, Göring managing to flee to Sweden.

Both served jail sentences at Landsberg prison where Hess, acting as Hitler's secretary, assisted in the writing of *Mein Kampf*. On release from prison, Hess continued as Hitler's personal secretary, and in 1932 Hitler rewarded Hess for his devotion by appointing him Chairman of the Central Political Commission of the Nazi Party, and gave him the rank of SS General. A year later Hitler made Hess the Deputy Führer, and Hess was further honoured by being named Hitler's successor but one after Göring. Despite these important titles and close position to Hitler, Hess did not have any serious political power. He was completely subservient to Hitler, and lacked the drive for power that other high ranking Nazi officers showed. It could be said that Hess was a servile sycophant who was obsessed with Adolf Hitler. Hitler, however, was beginning to distance himself from Hess, and favoured the stronger Nazi officers such as Göring, Himmler, and Goebbels. It may have been a desperate attempt to regain Hitler's affection that prompted Hess to make a solo flight to Britain. However the reasons for his extraordinary flight will never be known with absolute certainty.

On 10 May 1941 Rudolf Hess took a Messerschmitt ME-110 on a five hour flight across the North Sea. His aircraft was detected by British military surveillance, and at 22.34 hours RAF Ayr in Scotland reported the aircraft as a hostile raid. At 23.06 hours a report came that Hess's plane had crashed near Eaglesham on Fenwich Moor in Scotland. Hess was found by a local man, David McClean, who handed Hess over to the Home Guard. At this point Hess had not revealed his true identity, using instead the alias of Alfred Horn. Hess announced 'I have an important message for the Duke of Hamilton.' Hess claimed to be a friend of the duke, and that the two had met at the 1936 Berlin Olympics. There is a theory that Hess wanted to see the duke as he believed that Hamilton was not a supporter of Churchill. Hess might have wanted to use the duke to influence the king to sack Winston Churchill as Prime Minister, the thought being that without Churchill the British would seek a truce with Nazi Germany. Hess went as far as to promise that Germany under Hitler would leave the British Empire unmolested on condition that Britain allowed Germany to occupy all of Continental Europe. Hess even threatened to starve Britain with a blockade surrounding the British Isles if this alliance did not occur. Another suggested reason for Hess's flight was that a few days earlier he heard Hitler announcing the date when Nazi Germany would attack Russia. Hess knew that this would stretch German resources, as they would be fighting a battle on the eastern front with the Russians whilst fighting Britain in the west. If Britain could be won over with promises of peace with Germany, the Nazi troops could concentrate on defeating the communist Russians. Of course his foray could be due to a combination of all three reasons — gaining favour with Hitler, getting the British on side, and defeating Russia. There is debate whether Hitler knew of Hess's intentions to fly to Britain to try to secure a peace treaty, but general consensus seems to be that Hitler knew nothing of Hess's plan, and was furious upon learning of it. Hitler stripped Hess of all rank and title, declared Hess insane, and even expelled him from the Nazi Party.

Whatever reason Hess had to inspire him to make the journey, numerous theories have been advanced. A letter held in the National Archives addressed to the 'Honourable Herbert Morrison, Minister of Information, London' was sent by a Canadian citizen not long after Hess's detention. The writer, too 'was desirous of finding out the true motive behind Herr Rudolf Hess's flight to Scotland, and I am happy to say, that it was conveyed to me by One of the Eastern Adepts through telepathic communication ...[fearing a revolution in Germany] Hitler and his most intimate circle ... decided to go over to England and give themselves up'. To test the reception they would receive, the correspondent says that Hess was to try it first. The letter was annotated with a laconic comment added by a Lieutenant Colonel: 'You may feel inclined to cultivate the writer who appears to have evolved a delightfully simple method of obtaining vital information! It is perhaps unfortunate that he did not consult the Eastern Adepts as to the name of the Minister of Information' (who would have been either Alfred Duff Cooper or Brendan Bracken, the letter is undated.)

In the meantime, Hess's arrival in Scotland was stretching British military protocol. The Home Guard at Giffnock quickly handed Hess over to the Army at Maryhill Barracks, to where Major Barrie was headed to take charge. He found matters not to his liking: only one member of the Guard was properly dressed, the

Rudolf Hess

lance corporal was dressed only in his shirt, trousers and braces, second-lieutenant B. Fulton was found in his pyjamas still in bed from where he was trying to make the necessary arrangements for Hess to be taken to hospital to inspect a suspected ankle injury, whilst second-lieutenant Bailey was dressed in tartan slacks and glengarry, all of which Barrie considered 'incorrect for the occasion ... [and] a discredit to the Army and particularly the Highland Light Infantry.'

From Maryhill, Hess spent a few days in the Tower of London before being transferred to the Prisoner of War Reception Station at Maindiff Court Hospital near Abergavenny, where he was to remain as a POW for the duration of the war. Hess's health was continually monitored at the hospital. He suffered from delusions, was convinced that the British Secret Service where trying to kill him, and often accused his keepers of poisoning his food. His doctors concluded Hess was half mad, although some still think that he deliberately represented himself as such. He certainly claimed to suffer memory loss, and would frequently refuse to talk. His apparent mental instability led to a suicide attempt on 4 February 1942, when he stabbed himself with a bread knife. By 1945 Judge Jackson suggested that Hess testify insane, and his case was heard by the Attorney-General.

After the war Hess was to stand trial at Nuremberg for War Crimes committed against Czechoslovakia and Poland and Hess was brought from hospital in south Wales to RAF Madley by armed escort. Margaret Dison was a Radio Control Officer at Madley and recalls that all staff were ordered out of the control room accept for Mr. Anthony Gerald Badman, the Senior Traffic controller that day. A few minutes later, six cars with armed military police arrived. Then Hess arrived in another vehicle escorted by more police. Mr. Badman recalls that Hess was lodged in the office in the control tower before being whisked away once the formalities were complete. Mrs. Rosemary Morgan was also on duty at the airfield, and recalls Hess being driven to the aircraft; he climbed aboard the plane and looked out of the window. Bessy Shackley, another member of the ground staff, also recalls Hess looking out of the window. The aircraft took off, and Hess was on his way to Nuremberg, where he was found guilty on all charges and sentenced to life imprisonment in Spandau Prison.

Further suicide attempts occurred in 1955 and 1959. He died aged 93 in Spandau in 1987, officially due to suicide by hanging. However, evidence on Hess's body suggests that it is unlikely that hanging was the cause of death, and that he may have been murdered. The conspiracy theories do not end there. The bullet scars on Hess's body were not observed during the post mortem, which has led to speculation that the man arrested in Scotland was, in fact, a double. This theory is further substantiated by the testimony of Hermann Göring during the Nuremberg trial. When asked about Hess, Göring is said to have replied 'Hess? Which Hess? The Hess you have here? Our Hess? Your Hess?' Was he a double? Did the real Hess die in the aircraft crash in Scotland? Was there some other explanation, even involving the British aristocracy? There have been many books written on the subject, but perhaps we shall never know for certain.

Recent Developments

On 2 December 1946 Number 4 Radio School officially ceased to be, and on 5 December 1946, all remaining personnel moved to Swanton Morley in Norfolk. The Mountain Rescue Unit established at Madley found a new home at RAF St Albans. In 1947 the ATC Gliding School briefly took over the Madley site, but the station was abandoned in January 1947, the site remaining Air Ministry property until the 1950s. In April 1952 the RAF used the empty hangars to store aircraft spares as a sub-site of Number 25 M U based at Hartlebury. That unit was short of storage space due to the rapid expansion of personnel and equipment caused by the Korean War. When the RAF finally decided to leave Madley the land was offered back to the original land owner, Mr. Donald Parsons. Some of the buildings were used to house poultry, and there are still poultry houses along Stoney Street. An attempt was made to remove the old runways, but they proved too difficult to excavate, and parts of it can still be seen.

In 1954 Madley was finally connected to the electricity national grid. People had to learn how to use such a new commodity, and the Madley branch of the Women's Institute provided lessons for the local ladies teaching them how to cook on new electric stoves. With electricity came a steady growth in population, and a new school was needed. Whilst it was being constructed the school used a lot of the old Nissen huts on the former base as temporary classrooms. Some people also unofficially moved into some other of the Nissen huts on the site, having nowhere else to live. Hereford Rural District Council decided that the huts were not appropriate accommodation, so a new housing estate was built at the Kingstone side of the site. The huts were destroyed, but some of the brick buildings were converted into bungalows. The County Records Office holds the architects' drawings which detail the conversion of the old Instructional Huts. The drawings show the residential terrace bungalows which were adapted from Blocks 30 through to Block 38, though part of Block 34 would be demolished (see overleaf). The bungalows look a great deal more comfortable than the accommodation provided for the personnel of RAF Madley.

Some of the hangars have survived and light industrial companies now occupy three Hinaidi and two Callender Hamilton hangars. But the most obvious change to the site is the British Telecom Earth Station which occupies a large part of the former RAF base, and the satellite antenna dishes can be seen for miles around. There was already a satellite antenna station at Goonhilly Downs in Cornwall which was built in 1962, but as satellite communications increased with the popularity of telephone and television services, the Post Office (the forerunner of BT) needed to secure a site for a new Earth Station. They needed a place where there was not too much electrical or radio interference which would be picked up by the sensitive antenna, and also a location where the satellite dishes could receive the signals of orbiting satellites over both the Atlantic and Indian Oceans, a requirement that ruled out Scotland, the north of England, most of Wales and half of Cornwall. The satellite dishes are extremely large and heavy, but are also very sensitive and require firm, stable foundations. The bedrock that was suitably strong to

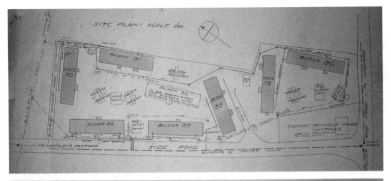

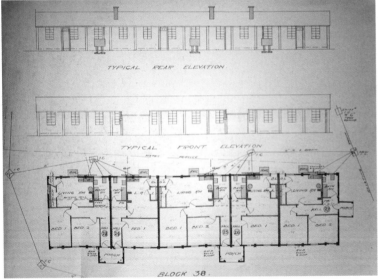

Plans for the conversion of the Instructional Huts into bungalows, showing the overall layout (top) and detailed plans for the conversion of Hut 38. (HRO MSB/156/93 & 94)

withstand the weight of the runways of RAF Madley was also suitable for the dishes. After a three-year search the Post Office secured the site in 1973 when they purchased 140 acres for £1,000 per acre. In 1986 a further 70 acres was procured to enable the Earth Station to expand. During construction occasional relics from the site's RAF past were found, such as the discovery of a bomb shelter. Finally in 1978 the Earth Station opened with just one satellite antenna dish. The dish continued in the tradition of the RAF wireless operators as it received and transmitted communications, this time not radio but telephone calls. The dish moves only 4 inches back and forth, and is permanently aimed at a satellite over the Indian Ocean. Initially there were plans for a further five dishes, but today the Earth Station is home to over 70 dishes measuring from just 80 centimetres to the first, and the largest one measuring a huge 32 metres in diameter. The dishes carry signals for television, internet, and telephone. The station is probably the largest and busiest satellite station in the world and employs around 100 staff.

When the Post Office was negotiating the plans for the Earth Station, they agreed that the site would be accessible to local residents by setting aside an area of land to be used as a Nature Reserve. This area is managed to encourage wildlife, and foxes, badgers, water foul, birds of prey, and bats are frequently seen. When the Earth Station became the property of British Telecom, BT created a wetland area in 1994, alongside the existing pond. The pond system is fed by a small stream and together with the grassland area and woodland, a diverse range of habitats have been created in a small area. This made the site ideal for educational purposes, and British Telecom considered building

Stoney Street

Hangars

Industrial Estate

Hangars

Former Airfield

Sewage Works

Antenna 1

MESC Nature Reserve

Aerial view of Madley showing the BT Earth Station and location of various places mentioned in the text

a facility to encourage learning and nature based activities. The facility was not constructed; however a group of volunteers, mainly British Telecom employees, were determined to see an educational establishment on the nature reserve site. Together, the volunteers formed the charity Madley Environmental Study Centre in 2001, and British Telecom agreed to lease the charity 20 acres of land. British Telecom provided a building to be used as a classroom, and funding for an Educational Officer. The aim of Madley Environmental Study Centre is to provide education to people of all ages and abilities in all aspects of natural history and conservation. The nature reserve is visited by more than 2,000 school children a year, and the number is increasing. More recently, adult workshops have trained people in various aspects

Three images from the event staged
at Madley aerodrome in 2005

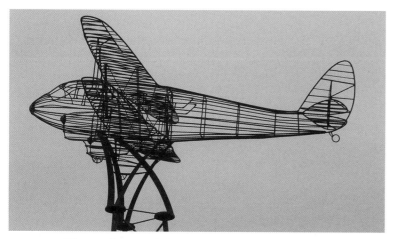

*The sculpture of the Dominie aircraft unveiled
at the airfield site in 2005*

public access to be used for educational and community based activities and events.

Madley Environmental Study Centre has been instrumental in celebrating the historical significance of the site. In 2005 volunteers worked tirelessly to organise a major event to commemorate the end of the Second World War. The event took place on the old airfield, and various RAF inspired attractions included a fly-over by helicopter, two impersonators dressed as Rudolf Hess and Winston Churchill, a Spitfire, and lots of war time memories, music and fun. Over 70 veterans of RAF Madley were able to attend the event, coming from as far as Cumbria and Devon. The event brought back many memories for those veterans who attended, and two WAAF friends were reunited after losing contact 60 years before. The highlight of the day was the unveiling of a permanent sculpture of a Dominie aircraft, by veteran Mr. Bill Williams. The sculpture recognises the tremendous work and sacrifice of all RAF personnel during those dark war years. We thank you. We shall not forget you.

of environmental management such as bee-keeping, making a wildlife pond, and species identification. The Study Centre is currently seeking funding to establish a facility with greater

The author, Fiona Macklin, dressed in a WAAF uniform, with Bill Williams, instigator of the research that has led to this book, at the event held at Madley airfield in 2005

Appendix 1
Daily figures of new cadets arriving on base and others posted off base

Key

F	French personnel		It	Italian personnel
Bel	Belgian personnel		NZ	New Zealand personnel

Date	Ground Crew In	Ground Crew Out	Air Crew In	Air Crew Out
14.10.41				
28.11.41	72			
30.11.41				
19.12.41				
20.12.41				
21.12.41				
19.02.42	74	59		
26.02.42	75	61		
05.03.42	75			
12.03.42	73			
19.03.42	75	75	299	
26.03.42	72			
28.03.42		50		
01.04.42	120			
09.04.42	120		55	
10.04.42		15		
11.04.42		60		
16.04.42	100		120	
17.04.42		40		
18.04.42		60		
23.04.42	100			
24.04.42		40		
25.04.42		75		
30.04.42	100			
02.05.42				60
07.05.42	100			
08.05.42			89	
14.05.42	100	64		
15.05.42			67	
21.05.42	100	56		

Date	Ground Crew In	Ground Crew Out	Air Crew In	Air Crew Out
28.05.42	100	56		
29.05.42			100	
04.06.42	100	70		
05.06.42			100	
11.06.42	100	77		
12.06.42			85	
13.06.42			15	
16.06.42				31
18.06.42	100	61		
20-24.06.42			97	
25.06.42	100	113		
26-28.06.42			101	
27.06.42				113
02.07.42	100			
03.07.42		105		25
04.07.42				50
07.07.42				25
08.07.42			115	15
09.07.42			17	
11.07.42				19
12.07.42				14
14-17.07.42			113	71
18-23.07.42			110	
29.07.42			67	
05.08.42			99	
07.08.42				75
13.08.42		84		
14.08.42				69
15.08.42				17
19.08.42			54	
20.08.42	60	108		
21.08.42				64

Date				
22.08.42				15
26.08.42			123	
27.08.42	60	81		
28.08.42				75
29.08.42				9
02.09.42			96	
03.09.42	60	48		
04.09.42				75
05.09.42				9
09.09.42			105	
10.09.42	60	35		
11.09.42				53
12.09.42				22
16.09.42			109	
17.09.42	60	80		
18.09.42				55
19.09.42				21
23.09.42			106	
24.09.42	60	21		
25.09.42				40
26.09.42				13
30.09.42			86	
01.10.42	100	26		
02.10.42				75
03.10.42				59
07.10.42			87	
08.10.42	100			45
09.10.42				21
14.10.42		50	146	
15.10.42	100	41		
16.10.42				50
17.10.42				44
21.10.42			161	
22.10.42	100	30		
23.10.42				60
24.10.42				18
28.10.42			279	
29.10.42	120			
30.10.42				50
31.10.42				18
02.11.42				62
04.11.42			48	
05.11.42	120			
11.11.42			140	
12.11.42	120			

Date				
13.11.42				34
18.11.42			103	
19.11.42	100			
20.11.42				33
21.11.42				60
25.11.42			12	
26.11.42	120		75	
27.11.42				60
28.11.42				15
02.12.42			130	
03.12.42	120			
05.12.42				10
09.12.42			99	
10.12.42	120	21		
12.12.42				62
17.12.42	120	25		
19.12.42				60
22.12.42				60
23.12.42				100
24.12.42	120	33		
30.12.42			87	50
31.12.42	?	54		
01.01.43				60
02.01.43				29
06.01.43	10		134	
07.01.43	110	70		
13.01.43			54	
14.01.43	120	55		
16.01.43				120
20.01.43			96	
21.01.43	50	71		
23.01.43				180
27.01.43			98	
28.01.43	50	109		
03.02.43			38	
04.02.43	50	108		
06.02.43				118
10.02.43			37	
11.02.43	50	27	15	
13.02.43				90
17.02.43			122	
18.02.43	50	11		
25.02.43	25	90		
27.02.43				140
03.03.43			91	

Date				
04.03.43	50	25		
05.03.43		67		
06.03.43				50
10.03.43			106	
11.03.43	50			
12.03.43		82		
13.03.43				60
17.03.43			101	
18.03.43	50			
19.03.43		98		60
20.03.43				30
24.03.43			87	
25.03.43	50			
26.03.43		87		
27.03.43				60
29.03.43			46	
31.03.43			148	50
01.04.43	50			
02.04.43		107		
03.04.43				60
07.04.43			202	50
08.04.43	50		35	
09.04.43		94		47
10.04.43				50
14.04.43			170	50
15.04.43	40			
16.04.43		79		60
21.04.43			127	40
22.04.43	50			
23.04.43		115		6
24.04.43				110
28.04.43		140		93
29.04.43	50			
30.04.43		109		
05.05.43			159	20
06.05.43	40			
07.05.43		115		
08.05.43				90
10.05.43				38
12.05.43			139	25
13.05.43	50			
14.05.43		118		
15.05.43				160
18.05.43				15
19.05.43			139	

Date				
20.05.43	40			
21.05.43		96		110
26.05.43			138	90
27.05.43	40			41
28.05.43		53		
31.05.43			110	
02.06.43			57	
03.06.43	20			
04.06.43		49		60
05.06.43				110
09.06.43			109	
10.06.43	109			
11.06.43		33		
12.06.43				30
16.06.43			101	100
17.06.43	40			
18.06.43		38		
19.06.43				60
23.06.43			146	
24.06.43	20			
25.06.43		50		55
26.06.43				84
30.06.43			100	
01.07.43	128	49	(Start of 'straight through' course)	
02.07.43				60
03.07.43				50
07.07.43	90			
08.07.43	128	40		
09.07.43				28
10.07.43				50
13.07.43	98			
14.07.43	168			100
15.07.43		46		
17.07.43				82
22.07.43	122	49		
24.07.43				38
29.07.43	5+135 straight through	50		
04.08.43	112			
05.08.43	61			
06.08.43		36		48
07.08.43				38
12.08.43	16			
13.08.43		49		

Date				
14.08.43				53
19.08.43	167			
20.08.43		36		25
24.08.43				76
26.08.43	124			
27.08.43		41		
28.08.43				90
31.08.43				101
01.09.43	85			
02.09.43	133			
03.09.43		39		20
04.09.43				30
07.09.43	38			40
08.09.43	13			
09.09.43	111			
10.09.43		41		
11.09.43				60
13.09.43				63
14.09.43				40
16.09.43	95			
17.09.43		41		
18.09.43				90
22.09.43	17			
23.09.43	57			
24.09.43		23		
25.09.43				45
29.09.43	14			
30.09.43	127			
07.10.43	219			
08.10.43		33		20
13.10.43	28			30
14.10.43	141			
15.10.43		24		65
16.10.43				96
20.10.43	16			
21.10.43	146			
22.10.43		50		
25.10.43	34			
26.10.43				13
27.10.43	6	8		
28.10.43	97			
29.10.43		40		
30.10.43	16			60
01.11.43	7			
03.11.43	8	22		

Date				
04.11.43	186			
05.11.43		88		
06.11.43		90		
09.11.43		12		
10.11.43	5			
11.11.43	116			
12.11.43		44		
13.11.43		20		
17.11.43	24	30		
18.11.43	152			
19.11.43		8		
23.11.43		23		
24.11.43	19			
26.11.43		34		
01.12.43	22			
02.12.43	118			
04.12.43		92		
06.12.43		30		
07.12.43		9 F		
09.12.43	104			
15.12.43	16			
16.12.43	141			
22.12.43	24 F			
23.12.43	120			
28.12.43		100		
29.12.43		12 F		
01.01.44		35		
04.01.44		30		
06.01.44	78			
11.01.44		76		
12.01.44		10		
13.01.44	84			
15.01.44		32		
19.01.44	24			
20.01.44	82			
27.01.44	90			
29.01.44		10		
01.02.44		13		
02.02.44		11		
03.02.44	63			
08.02.44		64		
10.02.44	102			
17.02.44	15 F			
23.02.44	21 F			
07.03.44		13 F		

Date				
08.03.44	100			
11.03.44	2 F			
15.03.44	100 + 16 F			
16.03.44		2		
17.03.44		1		
21.03.44		40		
22.03.44	100			
23.03.44		1		
25.03.44		42		
28.03.44		67		
29.03.44	100			
31.03.44		20		
04.04.44		124		
11.04.44		14 F		
12.04.44	6 + 39 F			
13.04.44	13			
18.04.44		82		
19.04.44	34			
24.04.44		75		
25.04.44		48		
26.04.44	2			
28.04.44	203			
29.04.44		2		
02.05.44		27		
05.05.44		10		
09.05.44		87		
10.05.44	37 F			
13.05.44		3		
16.05.44	70	53		
17.05.44	30	70		
19.05.44	61			
20.05.44		68		
23.05.44	13			
24.05.44		83		
26.05.44	215	62		
29.05.44		61		
30.05.44		123		
31.05.44		80		
06.06.44		173		
07.06.44	41 F	8		
09.06.44		51		
13.06.44	16 F	74		
16.06.44		53		
17.06.44		30		
20.06.44		68		
21.06.44		37		
27.06.44		99		
28.06.44	39			
30.06.44		8		
01.07.44	1			
04.07.44		19		
05.07.44	143 + 36 F			
07.07.44		80		
08.07.44	5			
11.07.44		58		
12.07.44	107 + 2 F	10		
13.07.44	13			
18.07.44		42		
19.07.44	13 F	11		
25.07.44		57 + 13 F		
26.07.44	152	4		
29.07.44		24 + 6 F		
01.08.44		60		
02.08.44	102 + 8 F	9		
08.08.44		79 + 1 F		
09.08.44	113	23		
10.08.44	87			
15.08.44		52		
16.08.44		7		
18.08.44	2 F			
19.08.44		28		
22.08.44		59 + 12 F		
23.08.44	60	8		
26.08.44	12 + 50 It			
29.08.44		6		
02.09.44		17		
06.09.44		7		
09.09.44	1 F	17		
12.09.44		12		
13.09.44		8		
14.09.44		109		
16.09.44		17		
18.09.44		18		
19.09.44	20 It	11		
20.09.44	5 F	5		
21.09.44	34			
23.09.44		21		
26.09.44		3		
27.09.44	13	9		
28.09.44	33			

Date				
03.10.44		38		
04.10.44	737	6		
05.10.44	34			
06.10.44		399		
07.10.44		13		
10.10.44		43		
17.10.44		10		
18.10.44	21			
23.10.44		81		
24.10.44		12		
25.10.44	23 F			
26.10.44		3		
31.10.44		20		
01.11.44	2	15		
04.11.44		41		
07.11.44		43 + 37 F		
14.11.44		21		
15.11.44	47			
18.11.44	2			
22.11.44	4 + 9 F + 15 It	10		
27.11.44		95		
28.11.44	3	8		
02.12.44		12		
05.12.44		42		
15.12.44	9			
16.12.44		27		
19.12.44		6		
20.12.44	2 + 10 F	8		
21.12.44	7			
27.12.44		20		
02.01.45		21		
03.01.45		25		
05.01.45	40	20		
12.01.45	17			
13.01.45		14		
16.01.45		32		
17.12.45	16 F	10		
18.01.45		14		
23.01.45		11		
27.01.45	7	6		
31.01.45	23	2		
01.02.45		10		
07.02.45	6	25		
09.02.45		66		

Date				
10.02.45		4		
13.02.45		13		
14.02.45	6 + 10 F			
15.02.45	2			
20.02.45	1	25		
21.02.45	27			
22.02.45		51		
24.02.45	2	2		
27.02.45	39	39		
01.03.45	380	10		
02.03.45	22			
05.03.45		13		
06.03.45		62		
07.03.45	19			
08.03.45		2 F		
10.03.45	3	24		
13.03.45		1		
14.03.45	8 F	20		
15.03.45	30	4 + 14 F		
17.03.45		90		
20.03.45		105		
22.03.45		3		
24.03.45		5		
25.03.45		17		
27.03.45		35		
28.03.45	17			
31.03.45		90		
03.04.45		45		
04.04.45	107	76		
07.04.45		3		
10.04.45		40		
11.04.45	118	20		
12.04.45		40		
14.04.45		93		
17.04.45		8		
18.04.45	80			
19.04.45	45			
21.04.45		29		
23.04.45	7			
24.04.45		47		
25.04.45	111	52		
27.04.45		6		
01.05.45		1		
02.05.45	118	14		
09.05.45	111	20		

Date				
12.05.45		14 + 5 F		
16.05.45	113			
21.05.45		10		
23.05.45	114	5		
30.05.45	28			
06.06.45	38			
09.06.45		9 F		
11.06.45		1		
13.06.45	25			
15.06.45		7		
20.06.45		3		
22.06.45	8			
23.06.45		3		
28.06.45	190			
06.07.45		23		
07.07.45		7 F		
13.07.45		79 + 11 NZ + 1 Bel		
18.07.45	38			
25.07.45	43			
01.08.45	16			
08.08.45	39			
22.08.45	39	725 ground redundant		
05.09.45	39	493 posted		

Date				
19.09.45	42			
18.09.45	1			
12.10.45	74	311 posted		
17.10.45	38			
31.10.45	76			
13.11.45	19	101 posted		
14.11.45	37			
19.11.45	1			
29.11.45	22			
04.12.45	1	93 posted		
05.12.45	11			
28.12.45	2			
29.12.45	2			
??.01.46	62	54		
??.02.46	91	373		
??.03.46	23	35		
??.04.46	0	374		
??.05.46	0	18		
??.06.46	6	151		
??.07.46	18	205		
??.08.46	73	208		
??.09.46	60	19		
??.10.46	?	?		
??.11.46	?	?		

Appendix 2

Number of personnel on base (monthly totals)

Date	Officers	Airmen & Staff	WAAF	Airwomen
31.10.41	?	438	0	0
30.11.41	41	844	1	0
31.12.41	58	1375	1	0
31.01.42	74	1378	?	0
28.02.42	79	1428	?	0
31.03.42	72	1928	27	0
30.04.42	77	2046	86	0
31.05.42	91	2448	92	0
30.06.42	96	3032	98	0
31.07.42	84	2649	5	103
31.08.42	93	2510	6	134
30.09.42	143	2562	6	91
31.10.42	92	3189	7	146
30.11.42	93	3838	9	203
31.12.42	?	?	?	?
31.01.43	92	3245	9	234
28.02.43	87	3883	9	268
31.03.43	84	3951	12	268
30.04.43	83	3651	13	368
31.05.43	85	3151	12	427
30.06.43	92	3236	11	437
31.07.43	96	3525	12	445
31.08.43	96	3688	11	456
30.09.43	97	3694	12	412
31.10.43	97	4095	11	386
30.11.43	100	4302	13	421
31.12.43	107	4506	12	424
31.01.44	106	4672	13	428
29.02.44	113	4621	8	424
31.03.44	122	4622	10	413
30.04.44	126	4612	10	418
31.05.44	135	4669	10	428
30.06.44	134	3998	8	450
31.07.44	125	4234	8	449
31.08.44	?	4124	?	466
30.09.44	131	3562	10	470
31.10.44	162	3756	11	475
30.11.44	172	3556	10	473
31.12.44	123	4132	10	478
31.01.45	144	1166	10	471
28.02.45	145	3565	9	465
31.03.45	162	3159	9	452
30.04.45	164	3044	10	448
31.05.45	164	3443	9	443
30.06.45	170	3356	9	445
31.07.45	178	3624	13	451
31.08.45	167	2995	13	423
30.09.45	?	?	?	?
31.10.45	144	3411	11	377
30.11.45	?	?	?	?
31.12.45	107	2401	8	346
31.01.46	116	2272	8	329
28.02.46	103	1943	8	313
31.03.46	99	1698	8	301
30.04.46	97	1394	8	258
31.05.46	76	1505	8	222
30.06.46	83	1096	8	205
31.07.46	73	667	6	130
31.08.46	65	738	6	133
30.09.46	56	520	6	101
31.10.46	55	423	3	78
30.11.46	49	481	3	26
02.12.46	Madley ceased, move to Swanton Morley			
31.12.46	47	465	1	0

Bibliography

Annett, D.M., *Saints in Herefordshire. A Study of Dedications*, Logaston Press, 1999

Bevan, Rev S.O., Davis, James, Haverfield, F. and the members of the Woolhope Naturalists Field Club, *An Archaeological Study of Herefordshire*, Nicholas and Sons, 1896

Coleman, Delphine, *Kingstone. Blanced Pence and One Hawk* Lapridge Publications, 1996

Cross, F.L., Livingstone, E.A., *The Oxford Dictionary of the Christian Church* 3rd Edition, Revised, Oxford University Press, 2005

Goodman, David Michael, *Archaeological Project*, held at the Herefordshire County Records Office, 1997

Hind, Maureen, *Madley Then and Now*, Logaston Press, 2000

History Directory 1858, held at Herefordshire County Records Office

House of Commons Journal Volume 2, House of Commons, 1641

Hughes, Philip, *Wings over the Wye, an Illustrated History of Aviation in Herefordshire*, 1984

Klausner, David N., *Records of Early English Drama*, University of Toronto Press, 1990

Leather, Ella Mary, *The Folklore of Herefordshire*, Jakeman and Carver, 1912

Richardson, Ruth E. & Musson, Chris, *Herefordshire Past and Present – An Aerial View*, Logaston Press, 2004

Roberts, W.J.L., *Aircraft Crashes Sites*, Brecon Beacons National Park, leaflet

Royal Commission on Historical Monuments, England, *Herefordshire Vol 1. South West*. His Majesty's Stationery Office, 1931

Smith, David J., *Action Stations: Volume 11. Military Airfields of Wales and the North West*, PSL, 1990

Sweet, Ted, *The Enemy Below*, Square One Publications, 1991

Watkins, Alfred, *Old Standing Crosses of Herefordshire*, Woolhope Naturalists' Field Club, 1930

Wilks, Mick, *Defence of Britain Project, Site Report*, held at the Herefordshire Sites and Monuments Office

Leaflet from Madley church

Internet Sites

http://groups.msn.com/Thethreemusthave Beers
http://members.aol.com/famjustin/Westonbio.html
www.breconbeacons.org/Frank%20Stokes
www.alliedspecialforces.org
www.lamp.ac.uk/celtic/Dubricius.htm
www.maryjones.us/ctexts/dubricius.html
www.worldwar2esraf.co.uk/Raf%20Stations/Madley.htm

Index